Pue
RICO

C000158037

The Caribbean

250 miles / 400 km

Dear Visitor!

Tropical rainforests, palm-backed sands, Spanish-flavored towns...Puerto Rico is a dream holiday destination. But this alluring Caribbean island also has an old and rich history that entices visitors away from beaches and Bacardi and invites them to explore. While winding mountain roads lead to secluded coffee plantations, ancient Indian burial grounds and one of the largest cave systems in the Western hemisphere, the art museum in Ponce yields works by European artists such as Rubens and Burne-Jones.

In these pages Insight Guides' correspondent in Puerto Rico reveals the surprising diversity of the island. He has devised a series of itineraries encapsulating the best of Puerto Rico, from the historic sights of Old San Juan and Ponce to El Yunque rain forest, the Cabezas de San Juan nature preserve and the rugged southwestern coast. His options include both the adventurous and the relaxing. They are carefully paced and include stops at characteristic haciendas, paradors and bars for refreshment and reflection.

 Larry Luxner lived in Puerto Rico for nine years, writing from his base in Old San Juan about Caribbean politics, business and culture for a variety of US publications. Writing this guide along with his wife Ani involved 'lots of hard work, sweat, sunburn, highway driving and a flat tire or two.' In 1995, the Luxners relocated to the Washington, DC area where they now publish 'South America Report,' a monthly business newsletter. They return to their beloved 'Isla del Encanto' whenever they can.

Hans Höfer
Publisher, Insight Guides

C O N T E N T S

Pages 2/3:
Palms at sunset

Pages 8/9:
San Cristobal
sentry box

Eating Out
An introduction to Puerto Rican specialties followed by a comprehensive list of recommended restaurants **78**

Calendar of Events
A list of all the main festivals in a Puerto Rican year **82**

Practical Information
All the essential background information you are likely to need, from climate to consulates, taxis to tipping.............**84**

Maps

HISTORY & CULTURE

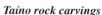

Puerto Rico's 3.8 million people enjoy the 'highest per-capita income in Latin America,' claims the local Government Development Bank. Meanwhile, tourist brochures call this 3,459-square-mile (8,958 sq km) island the 'travel bargain of the Caribbean.' Yet when politicians seek money from Washington, they remind Congress that Puerto Ricans – all US citizens – make do with half the per-capita income of the poorest American state, Mississippi.

What's going on here? Is Puerto Rico part of Latin America, part of the United States, part of the Caribbean – or all three?

That depends on who you ask. The island's official title is *Estado Libre Asociado de Puerto Rico* (which loosely translates as 'Free Associated State' or Commonwealth). But what does that actually mean? Is Puerto Rico anything like the Commonwealth of Massachusetts, a member of the British Commonwealth – or, as the former Soviet Union was known for a time, the Commonwealth of Independent States?

Certainly not. In fact, some people will tell you that *Estado Libre Asociado* – or ELA for short – is a complete misnomer since

Taíno rock carvings

Puerto Rico isn't associated, isn't a state and isn't free. The truth is that, culturally speaking, Puerto Rico has more in common with Cuba, Venezuela and the Dominican Republic. From an economic perspective, however, it is almost completely tied to Washington.

An Island Discovered

The island's status dilemma traces its origins to November 19, 1493, the day Christopher Columbus landed somewhere along Puerto Rico's northwestern shore (near today's Aguadilla) and claimed the island for Spain. At that time, Puerto Rico ('rich port' in Spanish) was inhabited by some 50,000 Taíno Indians, also known as Arawaks. Rock paintings left by the Taínos can still be seen at the Caguana Indian Ceremonial Park near Utuado and carbon dating of artefacts discovered in a limestone cave indicate that the island had been inhabited since the 1st century AD.

Juan Ponce de León

In 1508, explorer Juan Ponce de León established a small settlement at Caparra (near today's Bayamón), having been attracted by the native people's ornaments, which he rightly believed meant the island was rich in gold. But in 1521 – the year of his death – mosquitoes and cramped conditions finally forced settlers to relocate the capital to present-day Old San Juan. After a few years of peaceful coexistence with the Taínos, the victims of European diseases, Spanish settlers began subjugating the Indians, eventually enslaving thousands of them, ostensibly to convert them to Christianity but really to use them as free labor in their gold-mining ventures and other pursuits.

By 1540, the island's gold mines were exhausted, and the colonizers turned their attention to agriculture. As the Taínos died out, they were replaced – over a period of 300 years – with West African slaves brought across the Atlantic by Portuguese slave-traders under the protection of the Spanish crown.

Old San Juan's El Castillo de San Felipe del Morro, finished in the 1540s, provided the colony's first real defense against attacks. Those attacks, mainly by French and British corsairs, persisted throughout most of the late 16th century, and culminated with the 1625 siege by Dutch captain Boudewijn Hendrikszoon. This was an attempt to end Spanish control in the Caribbean, but it ended in defeat for the Dutch only one month after it began.

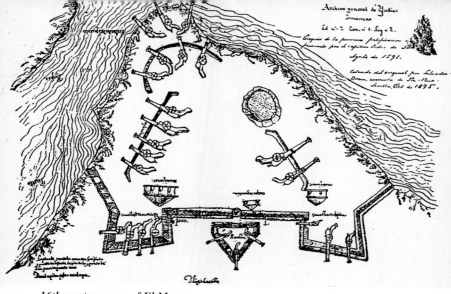

16th-century map of El Morro

In the 1630s, King Philip IV of Spain began fortifying the entire capital with seven fortresses linked by a line of sandstone walls surrounding the city. By 1765, according to a report by Alejandro O'Reilly (commissioned by Spain to investigate contraband activity), Puerto Rico's population had reached 45,000. This included 5,000 slaves and 2,000 pure-blooded Taínos, most of whom earned a precarious living through smuggling. Following the French-Spanish declaration of war on England in 1797, a British fleet of 60 vessels manned by 9,000 troops attempted to take San Juan by force. It was forced to turn back only a few weeks later.

In 1809, shortly after the Napoleonic invasion of Spain, the resistance government took the first step towards democracy by inviting Puerto Rico to send one delegate to Cádiz. In 1812, the constitutional government went a step further and granted Puerto Ricans conditional citizenship.

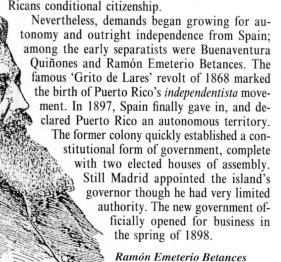

Nevertheless, demands began growing for autonomy and outright independence from Spain; among the early separatists were Buenaventura Quiñones and Ramón Emeterio Betances. The famous 'Grito de Lares' revolt of 1868 marked the birth of Puerto Rico's *independentista* movement. In 1897, Spain finally gave in, and declared Puerto Rico an autonomous territory. The former colony quickly established a constitutional form of government, complete with two elected houses of assembly. Still Madrid appointed the island's governor though he had very limited authority. The new government officially opened for business in the spring of 1898.

Ramón Emeterio Betances

But Puerto Rico's quasi-independence was painfully short-lived. On July 25, 1898, General Nelson A Miles landed at Guánica with 16,000 American troops, promising the people of Puerto Rico that 'We have come to promote your prosperity, and to bestow upon you the immunities and blessing of the liberal institutions of our government.' The Spanish-American War lasted less than four months, the Puerto Rico campaign only two weeks. When it was over, US troops were in Puerto Rico, Cuba, the Philippines, Guam and various Pacific islands.

Four years later, Cuba gained its independence; so, eventually, did the Philippines. Yet Puerto Rico – where the sentiment for independence was never strong – became a valued American possession. US troops lost no time converting Spanish military fortifications into American ones. Throughout the island, the Spanish *peseta* quickly gave way to the US dollar, and Spanish postage stamps were replaced by American ones (a beautiful mural of these early stamps can be seen in the main lobby of the Old San Juan Post Office).

The Foraker Act of 1900 formalized Puerto Rico's colonial status, while the Jones Act of 1917 made all island residents US citizens. But it wasn't until July 25, 1952, that Puerto Rico – as a result of forceful negotiations by the island's first elected governor, Luis Muñoz Marín of the Popular Democratic Party – voted to become a US commonwealth.

Under Muñoz Marín's leadership, Puerto Rico was gradually transformed from an agriculture-based economy dependent on sugar, coffee and tobacco into a world-class manufacturing center. Per-capita income, which in 1940 had stood at $121 – about the level of Haiti – now exceeded that of most South American countries. By 1955, manufacturing for the first time surpassed agriculture in importance. The economic development program, called 'Operation Bootstrap' and based on US tax incentives, attracted interest from many Third World countries keen to emulate it.

The Spanish-American War

But not everyone was happy with the pro-American direction Puerto Rico was taking. In 1950, Puerto Rican extremists, led by Pedro Albizu Campos, tried to assassinate President Harry S Truman in Washington; back home, revolts flared in several island towns. Four years later, members of the same group opened fire in the US House of Representatives' visitors gallery, wounding five Congressmen.

Puerto Rican–US tensions in 'West Side Story'

Nevertheless, the Nationalists – and the *macheteros* or violent supporters of independence who followed them – have traditionally been a very small segment of island society; the vast majority of Puerto Ricans favor close ties with the United States.

Under commonwealth status (reaffirmed by voters in the 1967 plebiscite and again in 1993), Puerto Ricans are exempt from US federal income tax, though they do pay personal income taxes to their own government and are subject to the US army draft. If anything, they are over-represented in the armed forces. As is cited by those in favor of statehood, more Puerto Ricans died in Vietnam per-capita than soldiers from any state – all having been sent there by a president for whom none of them had voted. And in 1993, the first US casualty in the war in Somalia was Puerto Rican.

State of the Nation

Because of traditionally high birth rates and medical advances that caused the death rate to plummet shortly after the Spanish-American War, Puerto Rico's population jumped to over 1 million by 1900. Today, its population density of 1,100 people per square mile is among the world's highest – only Bangladesh, The Maldives, Barbados, Taiwan, South Korea and the city-states of Hong Kong and Singapore are more crowded.

For administrative purposes, Puerto Rico is divided into 78 distinct municipalities. They range in size from Arecibo and Ponce, with more than 100 square miles each, to six-square-mile Cataño, home of the Bacardi rum distillery. Population-wise, the largest *municipio* is San Juan, with more than 430,000 people; the smallest is offshore Culebra, with less than 2,000.

Because Puerto Rico isn't an independent nation, there's no such thing as a Puerto Rican passport (although some radical independence supporters recently designed one after formally renouncing their US citizenship). Travel to the US mainland is unrestricted, and some 2.5 million Puerto Ricans now live in *'los estados'* – about half of them in New York City.

Yet because Puerto Rico isn't a state, island residents can't vote in US presidential elections. Strangely enough, they *can* vote in the Democratic and Republican primaries, which is why presidential candidates sometimes campaign here. Puerto Ricans also elect to the US House of Representatives, a resident commissioner who has a voice but no vote on legislative matters.

Two parties are fighting to change that. The New Progressive Party, led by current Governor Pedro Rosselló, wants to make Puerto Rico the 51st state. Under statehood, his party claims, the island would rapidly achieve economic parity with the rest of the United States while being allowed to keep certain vestiges of sovereignty, such as separate participation in the Olympic Games and the Miss Universe contest. This is no small matter in Puerto Rico, which is bidding to host the 2004 Olympics and has already captured the Miss Universe crown three times.

Beauty queens notwithstanding, Puerto Rico is unlikely to become the 51st US state until well into the next century. The November 1993 plebiscite showed that a slight majority of Puerto Ricans were opposed to the idea. (The actual vote was commonwealth 48.6 percent; statehood 46.5 percent and independence 4.5 percent.)

Nevertheless, *estadistas* still dream of adding that 51st star to the US flag, while – at the other end of the spectrum – the Puerto Rican Independence Party still dreams of a Republic of Puerto Rico free of US influence. These *independentistas* make lots of headlines but in recent years have rarely won more than 5 percent of votes in islandwide gubernatorial elections.

Besides political status, three other issues frequently confuse first-time visitors to Puerto Rico: language, taxes and the metric system.

For 90 years, the island had two official languages, Spanish and En-

A wave of political enthusiasm

glish. In 1991, former Governor Rafael Hernández Colón, citing Puerto Rico's 'cultural heritage,' abolished English as an official language – an act that won him Spain's Prince of Asturias award but sparked an outcry from many local educators and business executives. Rosselló, who took office in January 1993, quickly restored the official status of English, making Puerto Rico once again bilingual. Regardless of the law, less than a quarter of Puerto Ricans are completely bilingual; outside the big cities, you will definitely need a few basic words of Spanish to help you get around.

Taxes are another issue. Under Section 936 of the US Internal Revenue Code (the successor to Operation Bootstrap), American firms are partially exempted from paying federal income tax on profits earned by their Puerto Rico manufacturing subsidiaries. As a re-

15

sult, some 2,000 factories now operate throughout the island, churning out everything from Microsoft floppy disks and Hanes underwear to Carefree chewing gum and Star Kist tuna – all destined for the huge American market.

Yet the future of this controversial tax holiday is not bright. Congress recently slashed corporate benefits under Section 936 and is considering legislation that would abolish it entirely within 10 years. In the meantime 936 accounts for some 300,000 direct and indirect jobs and has helped give Puerto Rico a per-capita income of around $7,000, slightly less than Taiwan's. Virtually every family owns its own color TV; nearly all enjoy basic telephone service. Many thousands of others also own VCRs and cellular phones.

But perhaps the most telling measure of Puerto Rico's relative prosperity is the explosion of automobile ownership. Puerto Rico now has 1.5 million cars – nearly one for every two inhabitants – and consumes half the gasoline in the Caribbean, even though it is quite expensive, so people only drive big gas-guzzlers if they are more interested in appearances than economy.

Incidentally, driving here is on the right-hand side, unlike in the nearby US Virgin Islands, where motorists drive on the left. And that brings us to the final point: the metric system. This confuses some visitors at first, because speed-limit signs are posted in miles per hour (to accommodate the speedometers of American-made cars), but all distances are posted in kilometers, and gasoline is sold by the liter. No use pleading, however, if you're stopped for speeding; there's no confusion about the fines which are always issued in dollars. Good luck! *¡Buena suerte!*

A picnic in the shade

Historical Highlights

4500BC Archaic Indians arrive in Puerto Rico, probably from Venezuela's Río Orinoco delta.

AD200–700 Igneris people inhabit the island.

800–1500 Taíno Indian civilization flourishes.

1493 Columbus lands near Aguadilla, claiming the island for Spain.

1508 Juan Ponce de León establishes first settlement at Caparra.

1521 Ponce de León dies in Florida; settlement moved to present-day Old San Juan.

1539 Spaniards begin construction of El Morro fortress.

1598 Ginger replaces sugar as Puerto Rico's main cash crop.

1625 Dutch captain Boudewijn Hendrikszoon lays siege to San Juan; retreats after only a month.

1765 Spain sends Alejandro O'Reilly to probe illicit island trade; population estimated at 45,000.

1797 British forces under General Abercromby try to take San Juan; they retreat only a few weeks later.

1812 Spain grants conditional citizenship to island residents.

1868 'Grito de Lares' revolt marks beginning of the *independentista* movement.

1897 Spain declares Puerto Rico an autonomous territory.

1898 Spanish-American War; US troops land at Guánica, ending Puerto Rico's autonomy and bringing the island under American jurisdiction.

1899 Hurricane San Ciriaco devastates sugar and coffee industry.

1900 Foraker Act formalizes Puerto Rico's colonial status.

1917 Jones Act extends US citizenship to Puerto Ricans.

1937 Twenty Nationalist protesters are killed by police in the 'Ponce Massacre.'

1938 Luis Muñoz Marín forms the Popular Democratic Party.

1942 Puerto Rico Industrial Development Co established.

1948 Muñoz Marín takes office as the first freely elected governor of Puerto Rico.

1950 Nationalists try to kill President Truman in Washington, and foment revolt at home.

1952 Puerto Rico becomes a US commonwealth on July 25.

1954 Nationalists open fire in the US House of Representatives, wounding five Congressmen.

1960s Operation Bootstrap in full swing.

1967 Some 60 percent of voters choose to retain commonwealth status in islandwide plebiscite.

1975 Igneri and pre-Taíno ruins found at Tibes, north of Ponce.

1978 Police kill two young *independentistas*, sparking the Cerro Maravilla scandal.

1985 Governor Rafael Hernández Colón links Section 936 benefits to President Reagan's CBI program, preserving the benefits, provided that Puerto Rico funds development projects of $100 million a year in various Caribbean islands.

1986 A New Year's Eve fire at the Dupont Plaza Hotel kills 97; arsonists are blamed.

1989 Hurricane Hugo hits the island, inflicting heavy damage on Vieques and Culebra.

1991 Hernández Colón abolishes English as one of Puerto Rico's two official languages; Pedro Rosselló restores it a year later.

1993 In a November status plebiscite, voters elect to retain commonwealth status; five days later, Puerto Rico celebrates 500th anniversary of the island's discovery by Columbus.

O c é a n o

Isabela
Hatillo
ARECIBO
San Antonio
Mora
Quebradillas
Bosque Estatal
de Cambalache
Barceloneta
Laguna
Tortuguero
AGUADILLA
Bosque Estatal
de Guajataca
Bajadero
Manati
Bahía de
Aguadilla
Cordillera Jaicoa
Montañas Guarionex
Rafael Capó
Río Grande de Manatí
Pta.
Higüero
Aguada
Moca
Lago de
Guajataca
Arecibo
Observatory
Florida
149
Rincón
Río Culebrinas
San Sebastián
Dos Bocas
Ciales
Moro
La Cadena
Lares
Río Camuy
Cave Park
Bosque Estatal
de Río Abajo
Lago
Dos Bocas
Añasco
Río Grande de Añasco
Utuado
Caonillas Dam
Las Marías
Caguana Indian
Ceremonial Park
Lago
Caonillas
MAYAGÜEZ
Montañas de Uroyan
C o r d i l l e r a   C e n t r a
Jayuya
Bahía de
Mayagüez
Maricao
Los Rábanos
Adjuntas
Cerro de Punta
1338
Reserva Forestal
Toro Negro
Hormigueros
Reserva Forestal
Maricao
Monte Guilarte
1205
Bosque Estatal
de Guilarte
Villalba
Pta. Guajanibo
Sabana
Grande
Bosque Estatal
de Susúa
Embalse
Toa Vaca
Cabo Rojo
San Germán
Yauco
Tallaboa
Alta
Tibes
Ceremonial Park
Juana D
Boquerón
Palmarejo
Laguna
Cartagena
Laguna
de Guánica
Palomas
Guayanilla
Aguilita
Bahía
de Boquerón
Bosque Estatal
de Boquerón
Bahía de
Guayanilla
PONCE
Pole Ojea
La Parguera
Guánica
Pta. Jagüey
Bahía
Sucia
El Faro
Bosque Estatal
de Boquerón
Bahía
Fosforescente
Ensenada
Las Paldas
Bosque Estatal
de Guánica
Pta. Brea
Pta. Cabullones
Santa Isabe

M a r

Puerto Rico

7.5 miles / 12 km

Atlántico

Vega Baja
San Antonio
TOA BAJA
Bosque Estatal de Vega Alta
CATAÑO
SAN JUAN
Isla de Cabraz
Pta. Las Marías
Bosque Estatal de Piñones
Loíza
Suárez
Pta. Miquillo
Cayo Icacos
Isla Palominos
Playa Sardinera
BAYAMON
Pájaros
Santa Barbara
Canóvanas
Río Grande
Luquillo
FAJARDO
Corozal
GUAYNABO
CAROLINA
La Dolores
El Verde
Bosque Estatal de Ceiba
Naranjito
Trujillo Alto
Campo Rico
Mte. Britton 941
Yokahu Observation Tower
Ceiba
Isla Piñeros
Orocovis
Embalse Río Grande de Loíza
El Yunique (Caribbean National Forest)
Sierra de Luquillo
Comerío
Bairoa
Celada
Duque
Daguao
Pta. Casajo
Barranquitas
Cañón San Cristóbal
CAGUAS
Juncos
Río Blanco
Naguabo
Cidra
San Lorenzo
Las Piedras
Aibonito
CAYEY
Reserva Forestal Carite
Punta Santiago
Sierra de Cayey
Humacao
COAMO
Campamento Real
Martorell
La Plena
Buena Vista
Patillas
Mauhabo
Yabucoa
Pta. Yeguas
Coquí
GUAYAMA
Arroyo
Pta. Figuras
Bahía de Rincón
Salinas
Bahía de Jobos
Jobos
Pta. Petrona
Cayos de Barca
Bosque Estatal de Aguirre

Caribe

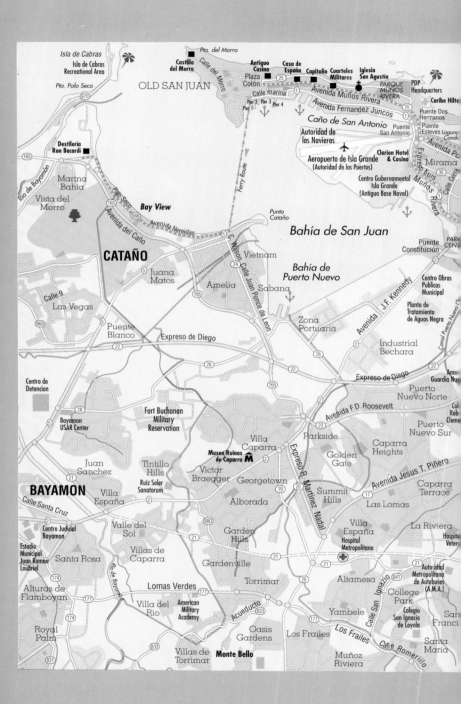

Isla de Cabras
Isla de Cabras Recreational Area

Pta. Palo Seco

870

OLD SAN JUAN

Pta. del Morro

Calle del Morro

Castillo del Morro

Pta. del Morro

Plaza Colón

Antiguo Casino

Casa de España

Capitolio

Cuarteles Militares

Iglesia San Agustín

25

PARQUE MUÑOS RIVERA

PDP Headquarters

Caribe Hilto

Calle marina

Avenida Muños Rivera

1

Pier 2 Pier 3 Pier 4

Pier 1

Avenida Fernandez Juncos

25

1

Caño de San Antonio

Puente San Antonio

Puente Dos Hermanas

Puente Esteves Lagu Cond

Destileria Ron Bacardí

165

Autoridad de las Navieras

Aeropuerto de Isla Grande
(Autoridad de los Puertos)

Clarion Hotel & Casino

Expreso Luis Muños Rivera

Mirama

35

Calle Carr

Rio de Bayamón

Marina Bahia

Vista del Morro

165

Palo Seco

888

Avenida del Caño

Bay View

Avenida Nereidas

6

Punto Cataño

Centro Gubernamental Isla Grande
(Antigua Base Naval)

Bahía de San Juan

Puente Constitución

PAR CEN

2

CATAÑO

Juana Matos

Vietnam

24

C. Wilson Calle Juan Ponce de Leon

Amelia

Sabana

Bahía de Puerto Nuevo

Centro Obras Publicas Municipal

Planta de Tratamiento de Aguas Negra

Canal Puerto Nuevo Ca

Calle 9

Las Vegas

869

165

Zona Portuaria

Avenida J.F. Kennedy

Industrial Bechara

22

Ame Guardia N

5

Puente Blanco

Expreso de Diego

28

22

2

Expreso de Diego

165

Puerto Nuevo Norte

Puerto Nuevo Sur

Col Rob Cleme

Centro de Detencion

9

28

Bayamon USAR Center

Fort Buchanan Military Reservation

Avenida F.D. Roosevelt

23

Parkside

Caparra Heights

Golden Gate

Avenida Jesus T. Piñero

Caparra Terrace

Juan Sanchez

21

Villa España

2

Tintillo Hills

Ruiz Soler Sanatorum

Museo Ruinas de Caparra

Villa Caparra

2

Victor Braegger

Georgetown

19

20

Summit Hills

17

Las Lomas

La Riviera

Hospita Veter

BAYAMON

Calle Santa Cruz

Centro Judicial Bayamon

Valle del Sol

Alborada

Garden Hills

Expreso R. Martinez Nadal

Villa España

Hospital Metropolitano

21

Altamesa

Calle San Ignacio

841

Autoridad Metropolitana de Autobuses (A.M.A.)

College Park

Estadio Municipal Juan Ramón Loubriel

174

Santa Rosa

Villas de Caparra

880

21

Gardenville

21

21

Colegio San Ignacio de Loyola

San Franci

Alturas de Flamboyan

174

Lomas Verdes

177

Villa del Rio

American Military Academy

Acueducto

833

Torrimar

20

Yambele

177

Santa Maria

Royal Palm

831

833

Villas de Torrimar

Monte Bello

Oasis Gardens

Los Frailes

Los Frailes

Muñoz Riviera

Calle Romerillo

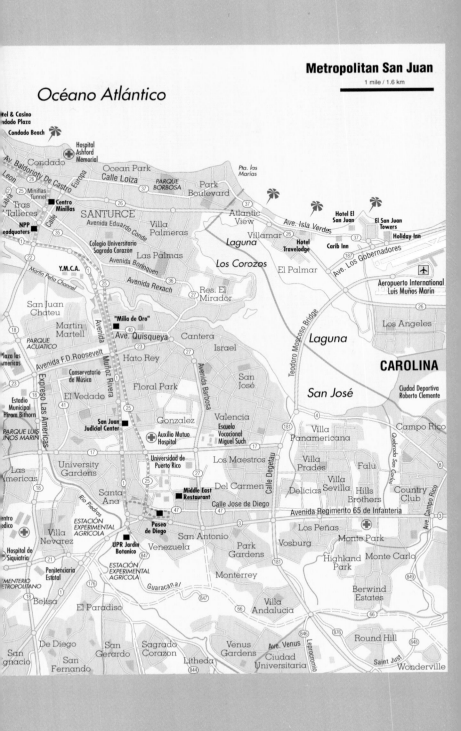

Metropolitan San Juan

1 mile / 1.6 km

Océano Atlántico

Hotel & Casino
ndado Plaza

Condado Beach

Hospital
Ashford
Memorial

Condado

Av. Baldorioty De Castro

Leon

Laura

26

Ocean Park
Calle Loiza

PARQUE
BORBOSA

Park
Boulevard

Pta. las
Marías

37

Minillas
Tunnel

2

25

Tras
Talleres

Centro
Minillas

NPP
eadquaters

35

SANTURCE

Avenida Eduardo Conde

Villa
Palmeras

Las Palmas

Avenida Borinquen

Colegio Universitario
Sagrada Corazon

Atlantic
View

Ave. Isla Verdes

Villamar

26

Hotel
Travelodge

Hotel El
San Juan

Carib Inn

El San Juan
Towers

Holiday Inn

37

Ave. Los Gobernadores

187

Aeropuerto International
Luis Muños Marin

26

Los Angeles

Laguna

Laguna

Los Corozos

El Palmar

CAROLINA

1

22

Martin Peña Channel

Y.M.C.A.

25

Avenida Rexach

36

27

Res. El
Mirador

26

San Juan
Chateu

"Milla de Oro"

40

Ave. Quisqueya

Cantera

Israel

27

Teodoro Mosqoso Bridge

18

Martin
Martell

Avenida Muñoz Rivera

PARQUE
ACUATICO

laza las
americas

Avenida F.D.Roosevelt

Hato Rey

23

Conservatorio
de Música

San
José

Laguna

San José

Ciudad Deportiva
Roberto Clemente

Campo Rico

23

El Vedado

Floral Park

Avenida Barbosa

Villa
Panamericana

181

4

Estadio
Municipal
Hiram Bithorn

41

San Juan
Judicial Center

Gonzalez

Auxilio Mutuo
Hospital

Valencia

Escuela
Vocacional
Miguel Such

Villa
Prades

Falu

8

PARQUE LUIS
JNOS MARIN

17

Del Carmen

Los Maestros

17

Calle Degetau

Villa
Sevilla

Delicias

Hills
Brothers

Country
Club

Quebrada San Carlo

Ave. Campo Rico

Las
Americas

University
Gardens

18

25

Universidad de
Puerto Rico

27

Rio Piedras

Santa
Ana

Middle East
Restaurant

Calle Jose de Diego

47

47

Avenida Regimiento 65 de Infanteria

Los Peñas

3

entro
edico

ESTACIÓN
EXPERIMENTAL
AGRICOLA

Villa
Nevarez

Paseo
de Diego

San Antonio

Park
Gardens

Vosburg

Monte Park

Highland
Park

Monte Carlo

1

Hospital de
Siquiatria

21

Penitenciaria
Estatal

UPR Jardin
Botanico

847

Venezuela

181

849

MENTERIO
ETROPOLITANO

18

Belisa

ESTACIÓN
EXPERIMENTAL
AGRICOLA

176

Guaracan a/

Monterrey

847

Villa
Andalucia

66

Berwind
Estates

66

San
gnacio

De Diego

San
Fernando

El Paradiso

San
Gerardo

Sagrado
Corazon

Litheda

844

Venus
Gardens

Ave. Venus

Ciudad
Universitaria

846

876

Leprocomio

Saint Just

Round Hill

848

Wonderville

San Juan & the North

San Juan, founded in 1521, is the oldest city on US soil and the second-oldest in the western hemisphere (Santo Domingo in the Dominican Republic was founded 25 years earlier). Originally confined to the seven-square-block walled area known as Old San Juan, the city experienced rapid population growth in the late 19th century. By the time of the Spanish-American War in 1898, many of the original walls were being knocked down to accommodate expansion to present-day Puerta de Tierra, Santurce and other outlying areas.

Today, there are some 1.5 million people living in the metropolitan area (which the local English-language radio station refers to at least a dozen times a day as the 'San Juan metroplex'). In addition to the Old City, this 'metroplex' includes Condado, Santurce, Isla Verde, Bayamón, Carolina, Cataño, Guaynabo, Río Piedras and Trujillo Alto.

View over San Juan

Decorated doorway

Besides being the political capital of Puerto Rico, San Juan is also the island's cultural, financial and nightlife capital. Sadly, it's also a mecca for criminals (the city's homicide rate is exceeded in the United States only by Washington DC), and it contains nearly half of Puerto Rico's estimated 10,000 Aids cases.

Despite its sprawled-out nature, San Juan's neighborhoods have managed to retain their individual characteristics. The hotels and high-rises along Condado's Ashford Avenue remind many tourists of Miami Beach, but Condado also has Spanish-style homes and stately mansions. Santurce, which has grown tremendously over the years, is still the city's commercial center, and more recently, a mecca for illegal immigrants from the Dominican Republic.

Slightly further inland is Hato Rey's *Milla del Oro* or Golden Mile, which has evolved into the banking center of the Caribbean, and Río Piedras, home of the University of Puerto Rico. To the east is Carolina and the San José Lagoon, bisected by the new $126 million Teodoro Moscoso Bridge − one of the largest public-works projects in Puerto Rican history.

The two full-day itineraries that follow will give you a more-than-adequate introduction to Old San Juan; the new city is then covered in a shorter morning itinerary.

1. Old San Juan

This full-day walking tour (*see* map on page 24) takes you from San Juan Bay along the Paseo de la Princesa to La Fortaleza, La Rogativa, Casa Blanca, Catedral de San Juan and Hotel El Convento. After lunch continuing on Cristo Street to Plaza de Armas for shopping. End the day with dinner at the island's oldest restaurant. (Note: La Fortaleza is closed on weekends.)

Begin at **La Casita**, a small building adjacent to recently restored **Pier 1** on San Juan Bay. La Casita, originally built in 1937 for the Department of Agriculture and Commerce, today houses a well-stocked tourist information center (open by 9am every day). Here you can pick up brochures, maps of the old city and the latest issue of *Qué Pasa*, a tourist guide published quarterly by the Puerto Rico Tourism Company. Ask for a free glass of orange juice, spiked − if you wish − with one of 17 varieties of Puerto Rican rum.

The **Plazoleta del Puerto** around La Casita is crammed on weekends with local artisans peddling leather goods, jewelry, paintings and ceramic figurines. Walk behind La

San Juan tourist office

Casita to the waterfront, passing the small black marble statue of Portuguese explorer Infante D Henrique (Henry the Navigator). Tied to the dock is *La Esperanza*, a tall ship built in Belgium in 1896 and refitted several years ago for charter tours around San Juan Bay – the Caribbean's largest cruise-ship and container port.

The pink building in front of you is the **Aduana** or US Customs House (closed on weekends). At the entrance to La Puntilla parking lot, make a left turn and walk down the street, passing **El Arsenal**, a former Spanish naval station, which is now a center for art exhibitions that change every three months (Wednesday to Sunday, 8.30am–4.30pm).

Return the way you came; straight ahead of you is the **muralla** or Old City Wall. There's also a large tourist map of Old San Juan (and one of Puerto Rico on the other side) to orient you. This marks the start of the **Paseo de la Princesa**, an elegant bayfront promenade that skirts the Old City Walls. Along this immaculate pedestrian boulevard, orderly kiosk vendors sell everything from cotton candy to *guarapo de caña* (sugar-cane juice). One dollar gets you an ice-cold glass of the stuff, crushed right before your eyes.

The Paseo de la Princesa, now closed to traffic, has been beautifully landscaped with towering coconut palms, leafy banyan trees, park benches, streetlamps and sculptures. One representative work contains five groups of sculptures symbolizing the five most important aspects of Puerto Rico's heritage: faith, liberty, sacrifice, society and cultural values.

La Princesa, on your right, was a temporary jail built by the Spanish authorities in 1837, with a tower and clock added in 1854. It

1 La Casita
2 El Arsenal
3 La Princesa
4 Puerta de San Juan
5 La Fortaleza
6 Museo Felisa Rincón de Gautier
7 Plazuela de la Rogativa
8 Casa Blanca
9 Catedral de San Juan
10 Capilla del Cristo
11 Casa del Libro
12 Centro Nacional de Artes Populares y Artesanías
13 Plaza de Armas
14 Alcaldía (City Hall)
15 Plaza de Colón
16 El Castillo de San Cristóbal
17 Museo de Arte e Historia de San Juan
18 Museo de Pablo Casals
19 Casa de las Contrafuertes
20 Plaza de San José
21 Iglesia de San José
22 Convento Dominican
23 Escuela de Artes Plásticas
24 El Castillo del Morro

Old San Juan
0.25 miles / 400 m

---------- Old San Juan
---------- Two Forts

Paseo de la Princesa

had the capacity to hold 270 prisoners, and was used as a prison until 1960. Following a renovation in 1990, it became the headquarters of the Puerto Rico Tourism Company. The hourly chimes emanating from its clock drift up to the streets running above. Inside La Princesa is a gallery exhibiting Puerto Rican art (Monday to Friday, 9am–noon and 1–4pm).

Continue along the *paseo* as it curves around San Juan Bay and an ornate sculpture and fountain, paralleling the 20-ft (6-m) thick ancient walls that have guarded the city since the 1700s. On the horizon, from left to right, are the Palo Seco power plant, the Bacardí rum distillery and Isla de Cabras, a long, palm-fringed islet with a Spanish fort.

After passing the small fishing pier to your left, you could continue walking along the *muralla* past the sentry box, but it's better to turn right at this point and re-enter the city through **San Juan Gate**. The gate was constructed in 1639, and during the 18th and 19th century was the symbolic entrance to San Juan. After disembarking at the dock below, according to legend, sailors proceeded through the gate to the nearby Catedral de San Juan, where they offered a mass in gratitude for their safe arrival.

But don't go to the cathedral just yet. Instead, turn right here and follow Calle del Recinto Oeste to the end. This is the entrance to **La Fortaleza**, one of Puerto Rico's most majestic residences and the oldest governor's mansion still in use in the western hemisphere. La Fortaleza (weekdays 9am–4pm) dates from 1533 and is Puerto Rico's equivalent of the White House. World leaders and other visiting dignitaries are always received here. In 1993, on the verge of the major status plebiscite, former President George Bush met with Governor Pedro Rosselló here to boost Rosselló's pro-statehood campaign. (Despite Bush's help, statehood was not succesful.) Guided tours of La Fortaleza and its impressive gardens are offered in English every hour, in Spanish every half-hour; proper attire is required.

La Fortaleza

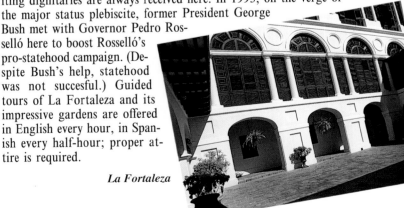

On your way out, you can make an optional quick stop at the **Museo Felisa Rincón de Gautier** (Monday to Friday, 9am–4pm, free admission), at the corner of Recinto Oeste and Caleta de San Juan. This little museum, is the former house of Felisa Rincón de Gautier, one of San Juan's most popular mayors. 'Doña Fela,' who recently died at the age of 97, led the city from 1946 to 1968; the house was later donated to the municipality and turned into a museum. It contains many articles belonging to Doña Fela, including her impressive collection of hand fans.

Back on Recinto Oeste, climb the steps to the top of San Juan Gate. To your right is the charming **Plazuela de la Rogativa**. This famous work designed by Lindsay Duncan, who lives on a nearby

Interior of Casa Blanca

street, depicts the bishop of San Juan followed by three torch-bearing women. It commemorates the *rogativa* or religious procession of St Ursula and her 11,000 virgins – held in 1797 during the British siege of San Juan. According to legend, the British mistook the procession for new reinforcements, and abruptly called off their siege.

Leaving La Rogativa, continue walking along the road nearest the water; pass through the gates and go up another road on your right. You might ignore the first little doorway on your right, exactly opposite the **Casa Rosada**, as just another hole in the wall. But it's not, and shouldn't be missed. Climb the stairs and lose yourself in the landscaped tropical gardens of **Casa Blanca**, mansion of 16th-century Spanish explorer Juan Ponce de León.

The residence (Tuesday to Sunday, 9am–noon and 1.30–5pm), was constructed between 1524 and 1530, specifically for Ponce de León, conqueror and first governor of Puerto Rico. From 1783 to 1898 it was the headquarters for the School of Military Engineers. Afterwards, it became an official US Army residence. Today, the Casa Blanca is home to two distinct museums: downstairs, a museum of family life in San Juan during the 16th and 17th century – including the throne room, the dungeon and a medieval kitchen – and upstairs, an exhibit on the Taíno Indians. Entrance is approximately $2 for adults and $1 for children and seniors.

San Juan Cathedral

Exit Casa Blanca by strolling through the courtyard and out to **Calle San Sebastián**. Pass Callejón del Hospital – one of only two step streets remaining in the Old City – and turn right onto **Calle del Cristo**. On your right, at No 52, is the **Center for Advanced Studies on Puerto Rico and the Caribbean**, originally built in 1842 as a religious school for young men. Numerous arts-and-crafts shops, antique stores and *gringo* bars crowd this picturesque street, which is frequently depicted on postcards and in watercolor paintings.

Also on Cristo is the **Gran Hotel El Convento**, founded in 1645 by the Order of Our Lady of Mount Carmel. The convent building now houses a 100-room hotel (free tours offered). Directly across the street is the **Catedral de San Juan**, where the body of Ponce de León has rested since 1913. The cathedral itself was built of wood and straw in 1521, but was destroyed by a tropical storm only five years later. It was rebuilt with Gothic vaulted ceilings and a circular staircase, and has been restored three times: in 1802, 1917 and 1973. Visitors are asked to make a small donation.

Walk all the way to the end of Calle del Cristo, passing, for the moment, dozens of upscale boutiques such as Ralph Lauren, London Fog and Gucci. This street, like many others in the Old City, is paved with *adoquines*, or small gray-blue blocks cast from the residues of iron furnaces in Spain, and brought over hundreds of years ago as ships' ballast. At Cristo's very end is the famous **Capilla del Cristo**. According to an old Spanish legend, this little chapel was built in 1753, in honor of a young man whose life was saved when his horse miraculously lurched to a stop rather than flying over the wall. On Tuesday (10am–3.30pm), you can glimpse the chapel's small silver altar dedicated to the Christ of Miracles. Next door is the enchanting **Parque Las Palomas**, a little park often filled with screaming schoolchildren chasing the hundreds – some say thousands – of pigeons who call this place home. It's certainly no picnic for those who live in the apartments above. From here, you can look out over San

Pigeons in the park

Juan Bay and see across to Hato Rey, Cataño and the distant suburbs of Bayamón and Guaynabo.

This is an good place to break for lunch. Half a dozen eateries crowd this end of Cristo Street, but none are as good as **Ambrosia** (250 Cristo), a sidewalk Italian resaurant-café owned by Ivo Bignami. Specialities include spaghetti in garlic and oil, chicken Ambrosia or filet of fish in wine sauce. If you're thirsty and want a delicious tropical drink, the folk at Crustaceo Delicatessen, next door, can fix you an orange, papaya and mango-juice frappe for only $3.50.

Across the street are two places of interest. The first is the **Casa del Libro** (Tuesday to Saturday, 11am–4.30pm, free admission), dedicated to the history of books and printing. Founded by Elmer Adler in 1955, this institution boasts nearly 5,000 rare works of all kinds including sketches, illustrations and ancient manuscripts – including 350 books written before 1501. Among the museum's most precious possessions are two royal mandates signed by Ferdinand and Isabella in 1493 (the so-called Catholic Monarchs) concerning provisioning the fleet of Columbus for his second voyage, during which Puerto Rico was discovered. It also possesses one of only six known copies of the first printing of the Third Part of the *Summa* of St Thomas Aquinas, dating from 1477.

Next to the Casa del Libro is another point of interest: the **Centro Nacional de Artes Populares y Artesanías** (Popular Arts and

Crafts Center). Run by the Institute of Puerto Rican Culture, this museum (weekdays 9.30am–5pm) houses a collection of island crafts which are displayed and offered for sale.

Come back up Cristo, and turn right at **Calle Fortaleza**. This is Old San Juan's premier shopping street; everything from T-shirts to butterflies in plastic displays can be found here. On your right is a dubious plaque claiming that on this spot in 1963, Don Ramon Portas Mingot created the *piña colada*. Others claim that an ingenious bartender at the Caribe Hilton invented the drink in 1957; no one knows for sure.

Walk one block on Calle Fortaleza and make a left at Calle San

A cheerful resident

José. This brings you to bustling **Plaza de Armas**, the heart of Old San Juan. Originally known as Plaza Mayor, this was the first square to be built in 1521 when the city was established. For the next 200 years, it was used as a military training ground – hence the name – though by the 19th century it had become a marketplace and center for official activities. Stone paving of the plaza began in 1840; it was completely remodeled in the late 1980s.

Today, several important institutions surround the plaza, most notably the **Department of State** – atop which flutter the flags of Puerto Rico and the United States – and the **Alcaldía**, or City Hall. The latter, built in 1604, underwent extensive alterations in 1841 under the supervision of architect Pedro Garcia, who tried, rather unsuccessfully, to pattern it after the Alcaldía in Madrid.

The Plaza de Armas is still used for giving public speeches and other official functions. Several commonwealth agencies such as the Office on AIDS Services and the Commission on Women's Affairs are located around the plaza, as are an abundant supply of fruit vendors, shoeshine men and beggars. Dominating the plaza's east side is **Pueblo**, the Old City's largest supermarket.

If you want to squeeze in some shopping, this is the time to do it. The streets all around Plaza de Armas – **Calle San Francisco**, **Calle Cruz** and **Calle San Justo** – are filled with galleries, boutiques and clothing stores of every description.

When dinnertime rolls around, you won't have to travel very far from here. Old San Juan certainly has no lack of fine restaurants – among them La Zaragozana (Spanish), Jalapeño's (Mexican), Le Chaumière (French) and Yukiyu (Japanese). If, however, you yearn for something truly Puerto Rican, **La Mallorquina**, at 207 Calle San

Justo, is a must. Founded in 1848, this restaurant is Puerto Rico's oldest business establishment, and supposedly the oldest restaurant in the Caribbean. That is easy to believe: the elderly, bow-tied waiters in immaculate suits seem to have worked there forever.

Try the house specialty, *asopao* – a rice stew spiced with native herbs and cooked with either chicken or seafood, and trimmed

La Mallorquina

with asparagus tips, tiny pigeon peas and red Spanish peppers. Also recommended is *arroz con pollo* (chicken with rice and kidney beans). Both dishes currently cost around $15. La Mallorquina always has fresh-squeezed orange juice and excellent Puerto Rican coffee. From here, it's an easy walk to Plaza de Armas and a taxi to take you back to your hotel.

San Cristóbal

2. A Tale of Two Forts

This full-day tour starts at Plaza de Colón and goes to Castillo de San Cristóbal via the Museo de Arte y Historia. After lunch, visit several museums, the Ballajá military barracks and the Asilo de Beneficiencia, before ending at El Morro. Buses, taxis and *publicos* stop at Plaza Colón (*see* map on page 24).

El Castillo de San Cristóbal (daily, 9am–5pm, admission free), plainly visible from Plaza de Colón, is marked at ground level by a large green 'National Park Service' sign. Both San Cristóbal and its more famous cousin, El Morro, are administered by the US government in Washington, a fact that makes Puerto Rican *independentistas* bristle with anger.

On the plaza's northeast corner is Hooters – an American-owned sports bar whose sexist motif has managed to offend Puerto Ricans of all stripes since its opening in 1992. Putting politics and morality aside for the moment, this marks the beginning of Calle Norzagaray, a picturesque boulevard that links the two forts and defines the entire northern edge of Old San Juan. Walk up this steep street (named for Spain's Lieutenant General Fernando de Norzagaray), past Hooters and the seven-story white apartment building on the left. At the crest of the hill, just before the road veers left, is the entrance to San Cristóbal.

In the parking lot, just off to the left, is a typical *garita* or sentry box. This is Puerto Rico's official symbol – just look on most license plates and you'll see one. Entering the fort itself, you pass wooden doors at least six inches thick, and a uniformed park ranger ready to help you with information and advice. As a nearby plaque says, this place – completed in 1772 – has the oldest European-type masonry fortifications in US territory.

Three flags dominate the large open courtyard in front of you – the American, the Puerto Rican and the 'Cross of Burgundy' used by Spanish fighting forces. The chambers to the left are gunrooms, some containing displays of cannons and other armaments.

Defending the fort

Off to one side of the courtyard are eight black cannons, while in the center is a small yellow chapel known as the **Capilla de Santa Barbara** – patron saint of artillery men. Continuing past the chapel, you'll come across the barracks themselves. Here, skillfully recreated, are barracks rooms complete with hanging uniforms and cots, and a scale model of Christopher Columbus's three famous ships – the *Niña*, the *Pinta* and the *Santa Maria*.

From here, you can take two paths up to the next level: a normal ramp or a cool tunnel. When you emerge, you'll see some black guardrails at your far left. This is an observation post added and used during World War II, when Puerto Rico was considered a strategic US outpost in the Caribbean. Looking out over the ocean from this very windy spot, you can see Calle Norzagaray wending its way past the slums of La Perla all the way to El Morro.

Along the precipice of the second level are two clusters of black cannonballs on display. Semi-circular iron tracks embedded in the stone are remains of a Spanish breech-loading cannon dating from the 1870s. Immediately to the right is a World War II 'fire control station,' where observers coordinated artillery fire for batteries along the Puerto Rican coast and reported the position and range of enemy submarines. From this level, looking back towards El Morro, you can see the six-inch Ordoñez cannon, which was unsuccessfully fired by Spanish gunners at the *USS Yale* during the Spanish-American War of 1898.

Allow at least an hour to see San Cristóbal. If you're feeling thirsty, stop for a rum punch at **Amanda's**, a trendy tourist hangout across the street from the fort. The restaurant is known for its *quesadillas* and other Mexican snacks. However, beware of slow service and notoriously high prices (around $5 for a margarita, plus obligatory 15 percent service charge). For a much cheaper treat, try a *piragua* (flavored ice) from one of several vendors who station themselves in this area.

Amanda's Cafe

Walking along Norzagaray, you'll notice several beautifully restored residences overlooking the sea. These are in sharp contrast with the tattered dwellings of **La Perla**, often discribed as the world's prettiest slum, which fringes the beach to your right. At La Perla's entrance are white concrete picnic tables under graceful palm trees, whose trunks are also painted white. Local residents gather here for ice-cold beer and community gossip. A ramp branching off from here goes down into La Perla itself – home to

Looking down on La Perla

about 1,500 hardy souls. No matter how picturesque this *barrio* may seem, don't be tempted to explore it. The area is known for drug-dealing and violence. Even longtime *sanjuaneros* rarely venture here. Tourists are advised to follow their example and appreciate the view from a distance.

Go up the ramp on the left, towards an arch labeled 'Casa La Providencia No 200.' On your left is a balcony crowded with sculptures. This is the unassuming entrance to **Galería San Juan** (Calle Norzagaray 204–6) – a combination of art gallery, museum and hotel so low-key that many locals don't know about it. Artist-owner Jan D'Esopo, who restored this unusual 400-year-old dwelling and took up occupancy in 1961, is one of Puerto Rico's most accomplished sculptors. She says her **Gallery Inn,** outfitted with antique furniture, homemade linen and hundreds of her own sculptures and paintings, is strictly for people who prefer the ambience of a private home.

The Gallery Inn rates vary from about $95 for a guest room to $190 for a suite with panoramic views (breakfast included). For an additional $1,500, well-heeled guests can even get their portrait painted by one of 12 artists-in-residence (busts range from $2,500 up to $40,000). If, however, all you want is a free tour of the place, call ahead, tel: 722 1808.

Further up on the left is the **Museo de Arte e Historia de San Juan** (Norzagaray 150, Monday to Friday, 8am–4pm). Even if you spend only half an hour, this museum – formerly a marketplace – is worth visiting for its interesting portrayal of Puerto Rican history through art. Norzagaray Street ends a few feet further on and becomes a pedestrian mall closed to vehicular traffic.

After leaving the museum, continue along the sidewalk that parallels Norzagaray, avoiding traffic. Descend the steps, turn left – going under the pedestrian overpass – and begin walking up unmarked Calle McArthur. On your right is the three-level **Plaza del Quinto Centenario** which looks out over the Atlantic. Dominating this plaza, at the center of an eight-pointed pavement design, is the **Totem Telurico**, a terracotta sculpture by local artist Jaime Suárez that symbolizes the blending of Taíno, African and Spanish cultures. Nearby is a fountain with 100 jets of water; it is supposed to symbolize five centuries of Puerto Rican history.

Walk past the large white building on your left, the Iglesia de San José (we'll come back to it later). Straight ahead of you is the **Plaza de San José**, a shady square that fills with teenagers on weekends and is the focus of Old San Juan nightlife. In the plaza's center is a large statue of **Juan Ponce de León**, constructed in 1882 from cannons captured during the unsuccessful British attack on San Juan nearly a century earlier.

32

Look up – the Spanish explorer seems to be pointing you in the direction of lunch. Several restaurants and bars line historic **Calle San Sebastián**; the best bargain is **Amadeus** (at No 105). Here, you can sample a delicious plate of *ceviche*, or marinated fish. Another house specialty is *ensalada romana*, a tasty salad containing romaine lettuce, Roquefort cheese, apples, walnuts and orange dressing. Other appetizers include fried *yautias* and plantains, while main courses range from a traditional American-style hamburger (the 'Jimmy Harrington burger' named after some unknown *gringo*) to chicken cooked in a wine sauce.

After lunch, return to Plaza San José and explore its many interesting sites, starting with the **Casa de las Contrafuertes** (House of Buttresses), the oldest private residence remaining in San Juan. On its first floor is the **Pharmacy Museum**, which recreates a 19th-century drugstore – scales, bottles and all; on the second floor is the **Latin American Graphic Arts Museum and Gallery** (both museums open Wednesday to Sunday, 9am–4.30pm).

Next is the **Museo de Pablo Casals** (Tuesday to Saturday, 9.30am–5.30pm), dedicated to the famous Spanish cellist and composer. He came to Puerto Rico in 1956 and founded the well-known Casals Festival the following year; the museum contains photographs and videotapes of previous festivals.

The adjacent **Dominican Convent**, dating from the early 1500s, houses the Institute of Puerto Rican Culture's music and book store (Monday to Saturday, 9am–5pm). Finally, enter the large white building dominating the square, the **Iglesia de San José** (daily, 9am–5pm).

The second-oldest church in the western hemisphere, the structure contains a collection of religious paintings, as well as a beautiful figure of Christ on the Cross and some ornate processional floats. Go across Calle del Cristo to the **Cuartel de Ballajá**, built as a hospital and later home to Spanish troops and their families. This is the centerpiece of Puerto Rico's recent $100 million program to restore Old San Juan in time for the 500th anniversary celebrations. A black granite tablet in Spanish entitled 'Barrio de Ballajá' offers maps of the area and explains how the building was restored.

Iglesia de San José

Inside the Museum of the Americas

On the building's second floor is the **Museum of the Americas** (Tuesday to Sunday, 10am–4pm), which seems to have just about everything from a replica of a country chapel to an exhibit on Haitian voodoo. From here, you can get a perfect view of the **Cementerio de San Juan** abutting La Perla.

Directly across the plaza from the Cuartel de Ballajá, along unmarked Calle Beneficiencia, is the stately **Antiguo Asilo de Beneficiencia** (Old Home for the Poor). This building (Wednesday to Friday 9am–4.30pm, Saturday and Sunday 9am–4pm) was built in the 1840s to house the destitute, and today serves as headquarters for the Puerto Rican Institute of Culture. Climb the stairs, go through an ornate foyer and enter the room to your left. Here you'll find an impressive exhibit on the Taíno Indians and artifacts from the Caguana Indian Ceremonial Park near Utuado, as well as from lesser-known sites in Jayuya, Guánica, Las Marias, Las Piedras and Carolina. On your right is a small exhibit of Puerto Rican *santos* or religious statues. Two huge interior courtyards are used for cultural activities; surrounding them are the institute's main offices.

Leave through the main entrance, turn left and follow the gravel path that leads straight to **El Castillo San Felipe del Morro**, which looms in the distance. The approach to the mammoth fort is a 27-acre (11-ha) grassy field, one of the few open spaces left in San Juan and very popular with kite enthusiasts.

About a third of the way to El Morro, on the left, is a 1925 statue commemorating the 300th anniversary of a Dutch attack on San Juan led by Admiral Boudewijn Henrickszoon. The September

Courtyard of El Morro

25, 1625 attack, repulsed by Captain Don Juan de Amezquita y Quixano, came 36 years after the fort's completion by Spanish engineer Juan Bautista Antonelli. Upon crossing a huge moat, enter the fortress, which was built in 1591, and continue to the inner plaza, surrounded by yellow and white walls. At this point, you can buy an audio walking tour, take a ranger-guided tour or simply explore El Morro by yourself.

Assuming you prefer the latter, keep walking past the gift shop and go right down a very steep tunnelled incline (there are 77 steps in all). This brings you to the third level. From the observation deck at this level, it's easy to see why few enemy ships ventured into San Juan harbor. The fort's guns were capable of aiming at any vessels within El Morro's field of vision. The walls themselves, connected with the system that circles San Juan, are 20ft (6m) thick. A small museum in the grounds of El Morro explains the structure's history, and the nearby gift shop has a nice selection of slides, postcards and books about Puerto Rican culture.

The gates of El Morro close at 5pm. Leave the fortress the same way you came, along the gravel path, but make a right at the large white building ahead, the **Escuela de Artes Plásticas** (weekdays 8am–6pm and occasional Saturdays). This building, finished in 1873, was originally an insane asylum. After Spain lost the Spanish-American War in 1898, it came under the jurisdiction of the US Army. In 1965, it was transferred to the commonwealth and eventually became the School of Fine Arts. Take a look at the various sculptures, paintings and

The massive walls of El Morro

other works in progress; more are displayed on the second floor. There's also a small cafeteria here if you're hungry or thirsty.

Exit the school, continuing along the same path towards San Juan Bay. This eventually turns left into a much shadier path lined with palm trees and other foliage. On your right – past the tennis court and several park benches – is the **Casa Rosada**, built in 1812 for Spanish troops. This little building was converted into officers' quarters in 1881 and someday is due to become a museum for Puerto Rican crafts.

Pass **La Rogativa** and **La Fortaleza** (both described in *Itinerary 1*) and bear left, walking up **Caleta de Las Monjas**, one of Old San Juan's narrowest and most beautiful streets. Finish the day with a drink at the charming **Gran Hotel El Convento** up on your left, where taxis are available to take you to your final destination.

An early-morning visit to the Capitol Building, Puerta de Tierra and the Hato Rey financial district, followed by a tour of the University's Botanical Gardens, a stroll through the Río Piedras marketplace and lunch at an Arab restaurant. You will need a car (*see* map on page 20–1).

This itinerary gives you a glimpse of the San Juan metropolitan area. Starting at Plaza Colón in Old San Juan, drive east on **Avenida Ponce de León**, one of the city's main thoroughfares. Along the way, you'll pass several historic buildings: the gray **Antiguo Casino**, built in 1917 and now used as a government reception center for VIPs; the large white **Office of Children's Services** building and the **American Red Cross** headquarters on your right, and on your left – all in rapid succession – the restored headquarters of the **Puerto Rico Olympic Committee**, the **Ateneo Puertorriqueño** (built in 1922), the **Carnegie Library**, the Casa de España and, finally, the inspiring Capitolio.

Try to find a parking space close to the Capitolio – but it may not be easy. Until a 900-car garage proposed by Governor

Columbus

Pedro Rosselló is actually built, vehicles are likely to be parked all over the place here, including sidewalks, curbs and even on the steps of the Capitolio.

Walk back to the **Casa de España**, an ornate structure built in the same 'Moorish Revival' style as the Serrallés Castle in Ponce. As you enter, notice the Arabic-inscribed enamel tiles along the base of the building. The Casa de España was constructed in 1935 and paid for by the Spanish expatriate community in Puerto Rico. Also see the tile painting of Don Quixote and, on the second floor, the Salon de Los Espejos (Mirror Room) with its painted wooden ceiling. The flags of Puerto Rico, the United States and Spain flutter from atop the building's blue-and-white Spanish tile roof, which is marred only by the presence of a huge satellite dish.

On your way out, note the stone fountain – a small replica of the Lion Fountain at the Alhambra in Granada – and walk back towards the **Capitolio**. This elegant building was designed by architect Rafael Carmoega and constructed between 1925 and 1929, though it wasn't decorated until the late 1950s. Ascend the marble stairs to the main entrance. In front of you, kept in a circular glass case resistant to humidity, you can have a look at the original 1952 **Constitution**, which was brought back to the island in 1992 after spending a full five years in a Washington restoration laboratory.

The Casa de España

Cupola of the Capitol Building

Directly overhead is the imposing cupola. The four corner sections, done in Venetian mosaic with gold, silver and bronze, depict some of the most important events in Puerto Rico's history: the arrival of Columbus; the island's colonization by Juan Ponce de León; the abolition of slavery in 1873, and the 1897 declaration of autonomy by Luis Muñoz Rivera. In the very center is the stained-glass seal of Puerto Rico, surrounded by figures representing science, health, education, justice and other ideals. A frieze located between the second and third floors shows in four panels how Puerto Rico's government evolved – starting with the Taínos and continuing through Spanish military rule to the arrival of US troops in 1898 and the island's establishment as a US commonwealth in 1952.

If you need refreshment, grab a coffee or juice at the downstairs Cooperativa La Rotunda, a subsidized cafeteria frequented by senators, representatives and local journalists. Then it's back to your car and on to the next stop.

The first traffic light after the Capitolio marks the start of **Puerta de Tierra** and more interesting buildings on the left, among them the **University of Puerto Rico's School of Tropical Medicine** and the **Puerto Rico National Guard Armory.** On your right is the unassuming editorial office of *El Vocero*, a sensational tabloid newspaper known for its bright-red headlines and gory crime photos. 'When you squeeze *El Vocero*,' say locals, 'blood comes out.'

Two large churches, **Nuestra Señora de Providencia** and **Iglesia San Agustín**, appear on your left, followed by the red-and-white headquarters of the pro-Commonwealth **Popular Democratic Party**, whose slogan is *Pan, Tierra y Libertád* – 'Bread, Land and Liberty.' Next comes the huge US Coast Guard station, protected by a barbed-wire fence, followed by the sprawling **Parque Muñoz Rivera**, famous for its shady banyan trees and its Peace Pavilion inaugurated in 1990 by Costa Rican President Oscar Arias Sánchez.

Monument in Baldorioty de Castro

Go over the bridge, get in the left lane and follow the arrow towards Carolina (Highway 26). You're now on beautiful **Avenida Baldorioty de Castro**, named after the early 19th-century founder of the Puerto Rican autonomist movement. A monument to the politician looks out over the Condado Lagoon. Across the lagoon are the hotels of **Condado**, while to your right are the condominiums of **Miramar**, an upscale residential neighborhood.

Following the arrow to Bayamón and Caguas, pass the **Centro Minillas**, a government office complex, and enter the **Minillas Tunnel** – the only one in Puerto Rico. Upon emerging, the big blue building looming out your right window is the headquarters of Governor Rosselló's pro-statehood **New Progressive Party**. Its slogan: *Estadidad es Igualdad, Seguridad y Progreso* – 'Statehood is Equality, Security and Progress.'

Exit at Hato Rey, backtracking in a big loop that takes you over the **Martín Peña Channel**, right past the *agua-guagua* water transport terminal and onto palm-lined **Avenida Muñoz Rivera**. You are now entering **Hato Rey** and the so-called **Milla de Oro** or Golden Mile, so named because of all the concrete-and-glass financial institutions that have established their headquarters here in the last 10 years. They include the biggest, **Banco Popular de Puerto Rico** – which celebrated its 100th anniversary in 1993 – as well as **Banco de Santander, Scotiabank, Eurobank** and **Chase Manhattan**. Most are in Puerto Rico because of Section 936, which exempts US manufacturers from paying federal income tax on profits earned by their plants in Puerto Rico. Some $15 billion in Section 936 funds are believed to be on deposit in the banks you see here.

Pass the large concrete **San Juan Judicial Center** on your left, and cross over **Jesus T Piñero Expressway**; this marks the end of Hato Rey and the start of **Río Piedras**, which used to be a separate municipality until it merged with San Juan in 1951. Follow this congested artery to the end, bearing left towards Carolina and Highway 3, and make a left turn at the sign reading 'Experimental C Guaracanal.' Make an immediate left at Route 847 and turn into the **University of Puerto Rico's Botanical Gardens**.

Water lilies in the Botanical Gardens

This sprawling oasis of tranquility – in the middle of metropolitan San Juan's most congested neighborhood – has 200 species of plants within its boundaries. A footpath takes you through the forest, past breadfruit trees, bamboo stands and towering Puerto Rican royal palms, and over an aquatic garden filled with papyrus plants and lilies. Admission to the park (weekdays, 8am–4.30pm) is free.

Coming out of the Botanical Gardens, bear right and make an immediate left under the bridge back onto Avenida Muñoz Rivera – but only for a few blocks. At the first traffic light, make a right onto **Calle Borinqueña** and drive up the hill. This is **Santa Rita**, a picturesque neighborhood inhabited mainly by students attending the nearby University of Puerto Rico.

At the end of this little street, make a left onto narrow **Calle González**, a right at the Burger King and another right onto Ponce de León (at the McDonald's). This brings you to the main plaza of Río Piedras, and on your left, the **Paseo de Diego**, a noisy pedestrian mall that comes alive every day with the sounds of thousands of shoppers and street vendors. Park in the underground garage and wander, taking in the sights, sounds and smells.

Only four blocks away from the main plaza is this crowded neighborhood's most interesting street: **Calle Padre Colón**, heart of Puerto Rico's small but vibrant Arab community (you may have to ask directions to find it). Most of the community's 2,000 or so members are Palestinians whose families came here in the early 1950s as street vendors and clothing merchants. On this street, storefronts display such names as Khami Rabi, Suleiman Imports and Jerusalem Inc. The Islamic Center of Puerto Rico, also located here, has main prayers every Friday at noon.

By now, it's lunchtime – and what better treat than an authentic Arab feast? Try the **Middle East Restaurant** at 207 Calle Padre Colón, where you can find homemade appetizers such as *humus* with tahini sauce, *falafel* or *tabouli* salad. For a more extensive Arab lunch, ask for the *shish-kebab* platter or *cordero relleno* (whole lamb with rice, pistachio nuts, garnishing and salad).

To leave Río Piedras, you have to get back onto Avenida Ponce de León. Pass the Auxilio Mutuo Hospital on the right-hand side, go back through Hato Rey, over the Martin Peña Channel and then make a left onto Highway 1, which will deliver you back to either Condado, Santurce or Old San Juan.

Shopping in Paseo de Diego

From Old San Juan, take the ferry across San Juan Bay to Cataño, home of the Bacardi rum distillery. After an interesting tour of the facilities, enjoy a complimentary piña colada, followed by a delicious seafood lunch at Palo Seco.

The 50-cent ferry from Old San Juan to Cataño is one of Puerto Rico's greatest travel bargains. From **Pier 2**, the ferry leaves every half-hour. During the 20-minute ride, you'll enjoy scenic views of Old San Juan and the suburbs of Guaynabo, Bayamón and Cataño on the other side.

Disembark and board a waiting *publico* to the **Bacardi rum distillery**, the largest in the world. The ride takes no more than 20 min-

Line up in the Bacardí distillery

utes and costs about $1. If you are driving, take Highway 22 to Bayamón. Before the first toll plaza, exit to Cataño (Route 165) and continue to the intersection with Route 888. The Bacardi plant is on your right.

More than 130 years after Don Facundo Bacardí y Maso distilled his first bottle of rum in Cuba, the company he founded has become a global empire, with plants in more than a dozen countries. Bacardi now accounts for 75 percent of US and 50 percent of all world rum consumption, with around 8 million cases sold every year. The company, which in 1988 went private after a family feud, enjoys annual sales of nearly $600 million, and pays about $200 million a year in federal excise taxes.

Bacardi offers free bilingual tours every 20 minutes (Monday to Saturday, 9–10.30am and 12–4pm, though it's best to go on a weekday so you can see the bottling line in production). The tour begins on the distillery's first floor, then up to the fifth floor for an exhibit of Bacardi products, and finally down to the second floor, where the production process is explained. From the distillery – which has a capacity of 100,000 gallons (454,600 liters) a day – tourists are taken by trolley to the Bacardi family museum, and finally to the visitors' pavilion, where you can sample free *piña coladas* and other drinks made with Bacardi rum.

Finding public transportation out of the Bacardi plant is a bit difficult, though a visit to the nearby **Isla de Cabras Recreational Area** is worthwhile. If you're more interested in a seafood lunch than a suntan, take a cab to **Palo Seco**, where you'll find **La Casita**, **Riomar**, **Boya No 4** and **Cain's**. From there, take a *publico* back to the Cataño docks and return to Old San Juan by ferry.

Although not duty-free, Old San Juan is well-known for gold, diamonds, jewelry and local crafts. Stores also specialize in imported objets d'art from Haiti, Colombia, Greece, India, Israel and the Far East.

Hato Rey's sprawling Plaza Las Américas, with more than 150 stores to choose from, ranks as Puerto Rico's (and the Caribbean's) biggest shopping mall. But if you want atmosphere, variety and a sense that you're buying something authentically Puerto Rican, Old San Juan is clearly the place to shop. Here, in this seven-square-block neighborhood so rich in history, you'll find a wide selection of handmade *mundillo* lace, carved wooden *santos* and traditional Puerto Rican musical instruments. In addition, many Old City shops are stocked with imported merchandise from around the world.

Although stores are located on almost every street in the Old City, the main shopping thoroughfares are **Calle Fortaleza, Calle del Cristo** and **Calle San Francisco.** During the day, cruise-ship passengers jam the sidewalks of these streets, especially on Mondays when half a dozen cruise ships are in port. Many of them follow tour guides who steer them towards specific stores – often for a nice commission on any purchases made.

Criticism aside, the **Puerto Rican Art and Crafts** store at 204 Fortaleza is one of the nicest and most tastefully decorated souvenir shops in Old San Juan. Here you can find carnival masks from both Ponce and Loíza in the $26–250 price range, butterflies in lucite for $10–50 and replicas of Taíno petroglyphs found at Utuado starting at $85. The shop also has beautifully framed prints with Puerto Rican political and artistic themes in the $100–600 range, and colorful hammocks starting at around $40. Only a block away is **El Artesano** (314 Fortaleza), which specializes in Mexican handmade crafts and original watercolors. Similarly, **Aguadilla en San Juan** (205 Cruz) offers a good variety of local merchandise such as clay Taíno souvenirs, Puerto Rican *pava* hats, *mundillo* lace and flags from around the world.

One of Old San Juan's most unusual shops is **The Butterfly People** (152 Fortaleza). The

Carnival masks for sale

walls of this gallery/restaurant are covered with thousands and thousands of native butterflies forever suspended in plexiglass. Towards the other end of Fortaleza you will find another unusual shop, **Moon Dance** (320 Fortaleza). Specializing in trinkets from the Orient, this store has everything from brass incense holders from India, to a statue of Krishna. Other items include beaded bracelets from Ghana, genuine Chinese iron balls and an 1895 African religious statue from Zaire.

You'll also find a taste of the exotic at **Machini Jewelers** (101 Fortaleza), which displays a collection of metal sculptures by noted Israeli artist Frank Meisler. **Leather Boutique Imports** at 56 Fortaleza offers a good selection of wallets, handbags and luggage from Colombia. Galleries along Calle Cristo sell everything from modern Puerto Rican art to Greek Orthodox religious icons dating back to the 18th century.

Clothing stores proliferate as well. **Tiendas Donato** (264 San Francisco) offers perhaps the Old City's widest selection of blue-jeans, men's shirts and suits, while the **London Fog Factory Outlet Store** at 156 Cristo offers unbelievable bargains on trench coats and other winter clothing.

Right next door to London Fog is **Spicy Caribbee** (154 Cristo), a quaint little shop that sells hot sauces from Vieques, Tortola and elsewhere throughout the West Indies. Owner Nereida Williams also

Spicy Caribbee's goodies

has a selection of teas, as well as candles and perfumes made from coconuts and other tropical fruits. The **Café Berlin** (on Plaza Colón), in addition to being a restaurant, is also one of the few places in Puerto Rico where you can buy organic salad dressing and natural maple syrup from Vermont. Just around the corner, on Calle O'Donnell, is **The Haitian Gallery**, specializing in vivid, colorful paintings.

Old San Juan also has its share of department stores. the largest of them is **Marshall's**, fronting Plaza de Armas, which has a wide selection of household merchandise and clothing at very good prices.

Tourists usually leave Puerto Rico with suitcases filled with assorted T-shirts, commemorative mugs, place mats and an array of 'Made in Puerto Rico' mementoes too numerous to describe. But the single most popular souvenir item has to be rum, and you may want to bring back a case of the liquid yourself. If so, visit **Barrachina** (104 Fortaleza) and choose from that store's extensive selection of Bacardi, Don Q, Ronrico, Barrilito and other fine Puerto Rican rum products.

Romantic promenade

6. San Juan Nightlife

An evening walk along Old San Juan's ancient walls, followed by a tour through the old city's bars and nightclubs. Alternatively, go to Condado/Isla Verde for something rather more glitzy. Here are Puerto Rico's biggest gambling casinos – the Condado Plaza, the Caribe Hilton and the Sands – not to mention the piano bars at the Ambassador, and Isla Verde's nightspots for unique local entertainment.

Now that the **Paseo de la Princesa** has been finished, it's hard to imagine a more romantic way to spend an evening than to stroll along this beautifully lit bayfront promenade. At night, Old San Juan's sandstone walls are illuminated with powerful yellow lights. This scene always reminds me of the ancient walls of Jerusalem – except, of course, for the giant cruise ships in the distance, and the ocean waves crashing on the rocks below La Fortaleza.

A nice stroll like this ought to be followed with drinks at **Café Violeta** (56 Fortaleza), an intimate bar with a beautiful interior courtyard, antique photographs on the wall and a baby grand piano no one ever seems to play. If it's Tuesday night, you might want to visit the old city's art galleries – all of which stay open until 10pm.

If, however, you need more excitement than this, Old San Juan has no lack of lively nightspots. **El Batey** (102 Cristo) is probably the island's most celebrated *gringo* hangout. Owner Davey Jones, cigar in hand, can be found behind the counter every night, shooting the breeze with his English-speaking bar patrons as a nearby jukebox blares everything from Lynyrd Skynyrd's 'Sweet Home Alabama' to the Beatles' 'Let It Be.' Covering the walls of this nostalgic little joint are framed caricatures of the owner's favorite customers, along with scrawled messages from thousands of

Having fun in Old San Juan

others who have passed through its doors.

Two blocks up Cristo, at the intersection of Calle San Sebastián, is the real heart of Old San Juan nightlife. A number of bars such as **Amadeus** (106 San Sebastián) and **El Pátio de Sam** (102 San Sebastián) are actually sit-down restaurants, while others like **Hijos de Borinquen, El Escenario, Boquerón** and **Aquí Se Puede** offer live entertainment and cater to a decidedly *independentista* crowd.

Old San Juan also has its fair share of teenage discos, including **Amnesia**, at 103 San Sebastián, and **Lazer's**, at 251 Cruz. The newest local addition, however, is by far the most impressive: the **Hard Rock Café San Juan**, which recently opened in a restored two-story mansion across the street from the Old San Juan Post Office. Here, Chuck Berry's guitar – along with John Lennon's jacket, Elton John's white wig and a closetful of other rock'n'roll memorabilia – cram the walls of this theme restaurant. In addition to the music, the food is great – if you can stand 150 decibels of Quiet Riot or Mick Jagger booming all around you. The Hard Rock Café 'veggie-burger,' complete with fresh garden salad, thick French fries and a glass of the best lemonade in town, is a bargain at under $10. After dinner, you can entertain yourself by reading early newspaper clips concerning the Beatles or more recent ones about Michael Jackson.

The disco crowd

More than a few locals have warned that all this emphasis on rock'n'roll will somehow endanger local Latin culture. To make sure no one's sensibilities are offended, Hard Rock plans to dedicate an entire wall of its restaurant to Puerto Rican musicians Tito Puente, Chayanne and José Feliciano.

Whereas Old San Juan is ideal for romantic walks, intellectual stimulation and funky *independentista* bars, flashy Condado and Isla Verde tend to bring out the Miami Beach in Puerto Rico. In just one 5-mile (8-km) long urbanized strip along the Atlantic Ocean can be found the highest concentration of hotels, casinos, nightclubs, discos and elegant restaurants anywhere in the Caribbean.

Every hotel likes to claims its entertainment is better than that of the others. Starting from Puerta de Tierra and going east towards the airport, they include the **Caribe Hilton**, with its outdoor orchestra overlooking the ruins of Fuerte Jerónimo; the fancy **Condado Plaza Hotel & Casino** straddling both sides of Ashford Avenue and connected by an overhead walkway, and the stately **Con-**

dado Beach Hotel, which looks like a beautiful mansion from the outside but has a reputation for bad service, unfriendly staff and general neglect.

One of my favorite places in Condado to spend an evening is the Cabaret Lounge and Piano Bar, which looks out onto the gaming room of the **Radisson Ambassador Plaza Hotel & Casino** on Ashford Avenue. There, pianist Joe Vallejo entertains guests with his renditions of 'En Mi Viejo San Juan,' 'Cuando Salí de Cuba' and 'Besame Mucho.'

To the east, past residential Ocean Park and a strip of guest houses catering exclusively to a gay clientele, is **Isla Verde**, a slightly newer version of Condado. Here can be found two of Puerto Rico's most luxurious resorts, the **Sands Hotel & Casino** and **El San Juan Hotel & Casino.** Big-name international performers like Joan Rivers and Liza Minelli perform at the Sands' Copa Room, while the lavish El San Juan is home to five award-winning restaurants including **Dar Tiffany** and **Back Street Hong Kong**, as well as a very chic disco, **Amadeus**.

For an equally enjoyable (and far less expensive) night out, stop in at **Lupi's** (Route 187, Km 1.3), a convivial Mexican grill and sports cantina that features friendly yet impeccable service, delicious *fajitas* for under $10, and an imported reggae band so good you may think you've landed not in Puerto Rico but in Montego Bay, Jamaica.

7. To the Rainforest

An early morning drive east of San Juan, via Piñones and Loíza, to the 28,000-acre (11,330-ha) Caribbean National Forest (El Yunque) and hike to the summit of Mount Britton. Lunch and afternoon visit to the Cabezas de San Juan Nature Preserve, a 316-acre (128-ha) park with spectacular views of northeastern Puerto Rico. Cabezas de San Juan is only open to the public on Friday, Saturday and Sunday, tel: 722 5882 or 860 2560 to reserve for the 1.30pm tour. See map on page 46.

Take Route 187 east from Isla Verde and Luis Muñoz Marín International Airport, following the signs to Loíza. Almost immediately, the hotels and high-rises seem to disappear from view, to be replaced by rustic beach houses and sand dunes. This is **Piñones**, a popular weekend spot among hard-working *sanjuaneros*.

From here, it is 16 miles (26km) and roughly half an hour to Loíza, through some of the most scenic Atlantic coastline Puerto Rico has to offer. Towering coconut palms and leafy seagrape trees stretch toward the horizon, unhindered by shopping centers or sprawling resorts.

Scenic stretch of beach

A Loíza local

Loíza, which was founded in 1719 and today has 29,000 residents, has the distinction of being Puerto Rico's only *municipio* whose inhabitants are predominantly black. This peculiarity dates back to the 16th century, when African slaves were sent by the Spanish crown to mine a nearby gold deposit. When the gold ran out, they became cane-cutters. The town's strongly African heritage can still be seen in its colorful and sometimes frightening carnival masks, for which Loíza has become famous.

Continue on Route 187 through another coastal city, **Río Grande** (population 46,000), and make a left at Highway 3; stay on this road for exactly 4 miles (6.5km) and turn right at Palmer. A sign directs you to the El Yunque rain forest, though it's still another 5¼ miles (8.5km) along scenic Route 191 to 'Cascada La Coca,' the waterfall which is El Yunque's best known and most photographed site.

You are now in the **Caribbean National Forest** – the only tropical rain forest in the US national park system. An estimated 100 billion gallons (454.6 billion liters) of rain drench El Yunque every year, giving life to hundreds of tropical species of plant and animal life, including the rare Puerto Rican parrot and the island's famous musical mascot, the *coquí* or tree frog.

Looking out at all the palm trees, ferns and Sierra palms crowding both sides of the winding road it's hard to believe that this

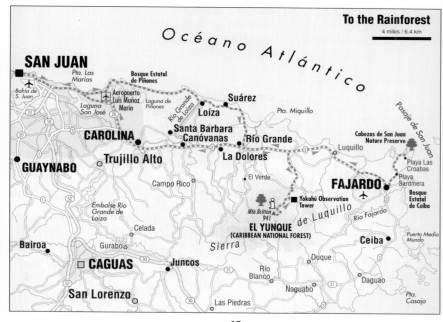

flora-and-fauna paradise was nearly wiped out on September 18, 1989, by Hurricane Hugo. The storm's 200 mile-an-hour (320kmph) winds left a path of destruction extending from the eastern fringes of San Juan to the offshore islands of Vieques and Culebra (not to mention St Croix in the US Virgin Islands, which was dealt a particularly punishing blow).

Two days after Hugo, I took a drive through El Yunque, dodging uprooted trees and downed power lines. The trip left me thoroughly depressed; I was sure it would take 50 years for the rain forest to recover. Surprisingly, though, most of the plants and trees grew back within two or three years, and today it's almost as if Hugo never visited the island at all. Some ecologists say that the hurricane actually helped El Yunque because it removed the canopy of darkness created by taller trees, giving smaller plant life a chance to flourish in the sunlight.

A storm of a different kind rages over Route 191, the road on which you are now driving. More than 20 years ago, a landslide forced the temporary closure of this road, making it impossible to drive all the way through El Yunque to Yabucoa near the island's Caribbean coast. The road was never reopened, and environmentalists are fighting to make sure that it never will be. They fear that a paved road through El Yunque would encourage US logging companies to set up operations here, destroying Puerto Rico's · last remaining rain forest.

Looming on your left is the 1,575-ft (480-m) **Yokahú Tower**, an observation point from which you can see Puerto Rico's north coast and the condos of Luquillo Beach. A little further up is the **Palma de Sierra Visitors' Center**; cold drinks and clean bathrooms are available here, but little else. The US Forest Service is currently seeking federal funds to build a $27 million tropical forest education center and 18 new trails, some of them leading into now inaccessible areas

Take Route 191 as far as you can. Just before the barrier informing you that the road is closed, make a right turn and follow the dirt path to a small parking area. A sign marks the beginning of the **Vereda Mount Britton** trail – an invigorating, 30-minute hike that takes you through breathtaking scenery. At the end of this slippery uphill trail is Mount Britton itself. The elevation here is 3,086ft (941m) above sea level, according to a

El Yunque

Mangroves in the water

brass marker placed at the top of the tower in 1941 by the US Geological Survey.

The 360-degree panorama from the top of this tower ranks as one of the Caribbean's most spectacular views. One minute, fog may obscure the huge radio antennae atop the very next hill; the next minute, the sky opens up and there are views as far as the bank towers of Hato Rey's Golden Mile. Conversely, this peak is visible from most of eastern Puerto Rico, and even as far away as the eastern island of Culebra.

After catching your breath and hiking back down, leave El Yunque the same way you came; several roadside stands offer delicious local foods such as *bacalaito* (codfish fritters), fried *yautias* and *parcha* juice (excellent for controlling high-blood pressure).

Return to Highway 3 and go east all the way to the outskirts of **Fajardo**, where you'll make a left onto Route 194. At the traffic light, make another left and stay on this road until the next traffic light, where you'll turn right. Pass through the heart of Fajardo, a somewhat cluttered city of around 37,000 souls which nonetheless boasts the charming little fishing village of **Playa Sardinera**. When you get to Route 987, turn left and continue until you reach the entrance to the **Cabezas de San Juan Nature Preserve** on your left-hand side.

Admission to this environmentalist's paradise ($5 for adults, $1 for children under 12) is limited to 224 visitors a day, guided tours only. The tour itself – available in English or Spanish – takes over two hours and is offered at 9.30am, 10.30am and 1.30pm.

Considering the incredible beauty of this 316-acre (128-ha) preserve, it's surprising that so few non-Puerto Rican tourists have taken the time to explore it since the park's opening in April 1991. Here, you can observe nearly all of Puerto Rico's natural habitats – coral reefs, thalassia beds, sandy and rocky beaches, lagoons, a dry forest and a mangrove forest. Sadly, about 80 percent of Puerto Rico's mangroves have been destroyed by development; this one, too, was supposed to be turned into a mega-resort, but was saved at the last minute when the Conservation Trust of Puerto Rico acquired the land.

The tour begins along a wooden walkway that takes you through a virgin mangrove swamp. Dozens of signs explain the animal and plant life you're likely to see along the way.

Next, your tour continues to the lighthouse itself – second-oldest in a series of 14 beacons built throughout Puerto Rico in the 1880s by the Spanish. This particular lighthouse, simply called **El Faro**, is on the National Register of Historic Places and has been restored using 19th-century techniques; the original copper dome and all original doors, windows and woodwork were spruced up in the course of the $1 million project. Today, the lighthouse – in addition to being an architectural gem – is an important venue for ecological and archaeological research; it also has several aquariums and an extensive marine biology lab.

The tour ends with a visit to **Rocky Beach**, which is made up entirely of corals and smooth black stones of every description. Swimming isn't allowed here, but just watching the foamy waves cresting in a semicircle, with the shimmering Atlantic in the distance, is reward enough for having made the trip out here.

At this point, you have two choices: visit **Luquillo**, one of Puerto Rico's most beautiful beaches, or **El Conquistador Resort & Country Club**, one of its most extravagant mega-resorts. If you choose

the latter, backtrack along Route 987 for about 2 miles (3km) to the entrance on your left. With 917 rooms and more than 2,000 employees, El Conquistador is Puerto Rico's largest hotel. Rates start at $385 for a standard room. The resort, first built in the 1960s, was abandoned at one point and later turned into a Maharishi university that soon went bankrupt; the

The pool at El Conquistador

reborn hotel was inaugurated in late 1993. Spread among five distinct themed areas, the complex features Moorish and southern Spanish architecture. The resort's exclusive Las Casital Village, which aims to "treat its guests like royalty," features a personal butler, private rooftop jacuzzi and VCRs in every room. The cost to stay here ranges from $800 to $2,500 a night.

If you opt for more rustic Luquillo, return to Highway 3 and head in the direction of San Juan. The palm-fringed beach will soon appear on your right. For a late-afternoon snack, try any of the 60 kiosks at the entrance to Luquillo Beach.

To return to San Juan, stay on Highway 3 and exit at Highway 26, following signs to Luis Muñoz Marín International Airport. This will bring you back to Isla Verde and the metropolitan area.

Lovely Luquillo Beach

This full-day excursion takes you along Puerto Rico's northern coast to the Río Camuy Cave Park, followed by lunch and a tour of the Arecibo Observatory. Río Camuy Cave Park is closed on Monday and Tuesday, and Arecibo on Saturday. Call the cave park, tel: 898 3100 and the observatory, tel: 878 2612, to check timetables and space availability and make sure you are on the road no later than 8am.

Anyone need a hubcap?

Take Highway 22 west from San Juan, following the sometimes confusing signs to Arecibo. Have plenty of quarters, dimes and nickels ready – there are frequent toll stops, and naturally, the *cambio exacto* (correct change) lanes are always much faster.

Until scenic Highway 22 is finished all the way to Arecibo, you will be re-routed to Highway 2 for at least part of the trip. From San Juan to Vega Baja, Highway 2 is the epitome of commercial clutter – telephone poles are covered with political propaganda and trees have been replaced with a selection of shopping centers, fast-food outlets, hubcap vendors and junked-car lots.

Further west, between **Manatí** and **Barceloneta**, come the pharmaceutical plants: Upjohn, Abbott, Bristol-Myers Squibb, Merck and others. All operate in Puerto Rico thanks to Section 936, the federal tax holiday that has become the centerpiece of the Puerto Rican economy. Originally designed to create jobs, many now call the program a waste of US taxpayers' money. No one knows how long Washington will maintain it, but for now its importance is enshrined in at least one nightclub along Highway 2 – 'El 936 Pub & Grill.'

After Barceloneta, the landscape opens up, and the emphasis shifts from factories to farms. This is the center of Puerto Rico's pineapple industry; several roadside stands offer delicious, fresh-squeezed pineapple juice for about $1 a glass (no sugar or water added) and whole pineapples for around $2.50 each.

Return to Highway 22, bypassing **Arecibo** – which is visible off to the right – and look for the Route 129 exit. Head south on this scenic road towards Lares, following the signs to the **Río Camuy Cave Park**. The park (Wednesday to Sunday 8am–4pm), is managed by the Puerto Rico Land Administration, and is on your left at Km 18.9. Entrance is currently $12 for adults and $10 for children, and this includes admission to all caves and sinkholes within the Río Camuy complex.

Breathtaking Clara Cave

You are now at the center of one of the most massive cave networks in the western hemisphere. Formed by the subterranean meanderings of the 350-ft (107-m) deep Río Camuy – the third-largest underground river in the world – this 268-acre (108-ha) complex includes three crater-like sinkholes and one cave. The ancient Taíno Indians considered these formations sacred; their artifacts have been found throughout the caves. Modern-day visitors, assisted by trolleys, lighted paths and bilingual guides, should allow two or three hours to see everything. It's advisable to wear rubber-soled shoes or sneakers, or else you may slip on the wet paths.

The park's main attraction is 170-ft (52-m) high **Clara Cave**, accessible only by trolley and only in guided groups. You must first watch a 12-minute video that explains park regulations. Visitors are then shepherded onto the trolleys for a 10-minute ride to the mouth of breathtaking Clara Cave. Impressive stalagmites and stalactites crop up all over this monstrous cavern, which has been preserved in the condition in which it was found.

Clara Cave and its surroundings were first explored in depth in 1958, by geologist Russell Gurnee and his wife, Jeanne Gurnee, a photographer. The couple's findings in later years are recounted in their 1974 book *Discovery at the Río Camuy*.

After returning from Clara Cave, take the trolley to **Sumidero Tres Pueblos**, named after its location at the meeting point of three *municipios* – Lares, Hatillo and Camuy. This heavily forested depression is 400ft (122m) deep and 650ft (198m) wide, but the closest you can get is a viewing platform high above the sinkhole.

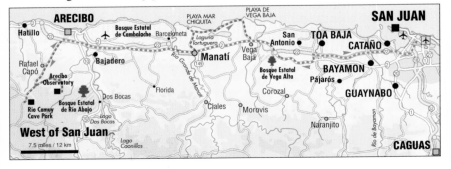

Spiral Sinkhole

You can, however, hike into the heart of the nearby **Spiral Sinkhole**, opened to the public in early 1994. Standing at the bottom of this unusual formation, a visitor – surrounded by the chirping of crickets, the cool breezes and the darkness – could easily be fooled into thinking it's nighttime. As a guide explains, it's called the Spiral Sinkhole because of the way in which sunlight entering it reflects the sinkhole's vertical walls. From the bottom of the cave looking up, you can see how light penetrating the cave illuminates its walls, giving you the feeling of being inside a giant snail. Through this sinkhole, thousands of bats leave the Río Camuy cave system every night in search of food.

The wooden walkway descending into the Spiral Sinkhole contains 205 steps – an easy hike going down, but a formidable challenge going back up, especially after such an exhausting morning. It could really work up an appetite.

Leaving the cave park, you have two excellent choices for lunch: **Restaurante Las Cavernas** (Road 129, Km 19.6) or **Restaurante El Taíno** (Road 129, Km 21.1). Both pride themselves on traditional Puerto Rican cuisine, bilingual waiters, family atmosphere and reasonable prices. At Las Cavernas, the house specialty is *arroz con guinea* (rice with guinea fowl), served with beans and *amarillos* (fried bananas). Both places accept major credit cards.

To get to the **Arecibo Observatory** after lunch, take Route 129 back north 2¼ miles (3.75km) to Route 134. Turn right at the Shell station onto 134 and follow the road through beautiful karst country for about 2 miles (3km). Continue 2½ miles (4km) along winding Route 635 and make a right at Route 625. About 2½ miles (4km) ahead is the observatory itself – so huge you can see it from a jumbo jet at high altitude, yet almost completely obscured at ground level.

The observatory (Tuesday to Friday 2–3pm, Sunday 1–4.30pm), plans to extend its visiting hours in 1995. Built in 1960 and administered by Cornell University, it has

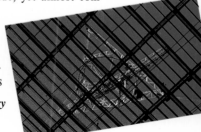

Arecibo Observatory

been the focus of numerous astronomical breakthroughs over the years, ranging from Alexander Wolszcan's 1992 discovery of planets outside our own solar system to NASA's recent $100 million Search for Extra-Terrestrial Intelligence. It gained international fame again in 1993, when the Nobel Prize in Physics went to two American astronomers – Russell H Hulse and Joseph H Taylor Jr – who did all their primary research on pulsars at Arecibo.

The observatory owes its existence largely to Puerto Rico's political status as a US commonwealth and to the island's geographic position 17 degrees north of the Equator. That makes it ideal for observation of planets, quasars, pulsars and other cosmic phenomena. The telescope is so sensitive it can detect objects 13 billion light-years away, just by systematically probing the depths of the universe with radio transmitters set at specific wavelengths and listening for their echoes.

The 'dish' itself, suspended over a huge natural sinkhole, is by far the largest of its kind in the world. Spanning 1,000ft (305m) in diameter, it covers 20 acres (8ha) and is composed of nearly 40,000 perforated aluminum mesh panels, each measuring 3ft by 6ft (1m by 2m). A 600-ton (544-tonne) platform, in turn, is suspended 426ft (130m) over the dish by 12 cables strung from three reinforced concrete towers. Underneath the dish lies a jungle of ferns, orchids and begonias.

To make the observatory more accessible to tourists, Cornell University is building a $2 million visitors' center, which – upon completion in 1997 – will include a 120-seat auditorium, a 4,000-sq ft (372-sq m) scientific museum with explanations in both English and Spanish, a gift shop and a trail leading to a viewing platform, from which the telescope can be seen at close range.

Leave the observatory the same way you came, though when you hit Route 134, make a right and stay on it until you rejoin Route 129. Turn right onto Highway 22 heading east towards San Juan. Shortly after it merges into Highway 2, make a left at Route 604 and follow it to the intersection with Route 685. Make a left again.

Atlantic coast

This takes you directly to **Playa Mar Chiquita** (little sea beach), a nice quiet inlet perfect for swimming, sunbathing and *piña coladas*. Alternatively, a right turn at Route 685 (which becomes 686 and then 692) takes you along the stunning Atlantic coast to beautiful **Playa de Vega Baja**, whose beach runs for 2,500ft (760m) from Boca del Cibuco to Punta Puerto Nuevo.

Afterwards, follow the signs back to Route 686, which connects to Highway 2 and San Juan.

Ponce & the South

To make the 75-mile (121-km), 1½ hour journey from San Juan to Ponce, leave the metro area heading south on Highway 18, passing the Caribbean's largest shopping mall, Plaza Las Américas, on your right, and later a maximum-security prison, nicknamed the 'Oso Blanco' (white bear), to your left. Highways 1 and 52 both go to Caguas. Bear left on Highway 52, and in a few miles you'll pass a blue sign in Spanish announcing "Welcome to the Luis A. Ferré Expressway," named after the 92-year-old founder of Puerto Rico's statehood party.

The large concrete-and-glass building on the right is the new headquarters of Citibank. Ahead on the left is a stylized *garita* or sentry box, marking the city limits of San Juan. Here, the landscape opens up to sweeping mountain views, giving you the feeling you've finally left the big city.

The 50-cent toll booth marks the beginning of Caguas, population 133,000 and the largest city in Puerto Rico's interior. The tall condominium on your left is Caguas Towers. Many pharmaceutical plants are located here. On your right is the turnoff for Cidra (Route 172), where Coke and Pepsi both manufacture their US supply of syrup concentrate under top-secret conditions. After the second toll booth (35 cents), look for the giant AT&T satellite dish to the right. Most phone calls to and from Puerto Rico go through this earth station. Next to it is the Consolidated Cigar factory, which employs 700 people.

Interesting highway signs now begin appearing, giving warnings such as 'Caution: Stray Cattle in the Roadway' or 'Foggy Area Next 12 Kilometers.' The black netting on the sides of mountains near the highway is designed to prevent rockslides.

Right before the *Area de Descanso* or rest area on your right is the Monumento al Jíbaro Puertorriqueño, a huge white statue dedicated to the *jíbaro* or country farmer. Around Km 53, the highway begins its descent from the mountains, and the Caribbean Sea ap-

Homage to the farmer

Taking to the hills

pears on the horizon for the first time. The landscape changes from lush to arid, and cactus trees dot the roadside. To the left of the third toll plaza (65 cents) is the sprawling Olympic Village, used to house athletes during the 1993 Central American and Caribbean Games.

At Km 76 is the exit for Santa Isabel. If you're hungry, this might be a good place to turn off for fast food. Santa Isabel, incidentally, is the site of an 800-acre (325-ha) farm where succulent winter tomatoes are grown for export to the US mainland. Many of the tomato slices found in McDonald's hamburgers come from here – maybe they are the best part.

Within 10 minutes, you'll see Isla Caja de Muertos (Coffin Island) rising from the sea to your left. Immediately after the fourth and final toll plaza (35 cents), take the exit to Ponce (not to the airport) and get in the right lane, marked 'Ponce Centro – Highway 1.' You are now on Miguel A Pou Boulevard. At the park, turn left onto Calle Isabel, the historic entrance to Ponce.

9. Walking tour of Downtown Ponce

This full-day tour takes in many important sites including the Museo de la Historia de Ponce, lots of interesting architecture and the Plaza del Mercado. After lunch, stop at Casa Armstrong-Poventud and the Catedral de Guadalupe and finally, the highlight of the day – visit Serrallés Castle overlooking Ponce. See map on page 57.

Picturesque Ponce

Named after Spanish explorer Juan Ponce de León and nicknamed *La Perla del Sur* (Pearl of the South), Ponce is Puerto Rico's second-largest city and among its most picturesque. The municipality, which today has a population of 190,000, was founded in 1692. However, the remains of indigenous Igneri and pre-Taíno civilizations at Tibes, north of the city, go back over a thousand years.

'Ponce is one of the oldest towns on the island,' wrote historian Iñigo Abbad y Lasierra in 1784. 'It is located on a big plain covered with trees...115 houses form an irregular square. The parish church [Guadalupe], which is small and deteriorated, is on one side; 5,038 souls live here.' From that humble beginning, Ponce grew to become, by the mid-19th century, the architectural, artistic and cultural capital of Puerto Rico. Enormous fortunes were made from sugar, coffee and rum – all exported to Europe through the port of Ponce. This gave rise to the various architectural styles seen today throughout Ponce, most notably the neoclassical *criollo* architecture which was introduced by Juan Bértoli Calderoni of Corsica more than 100 years ago.

Despite the wealth, Ponce also suffered a string of tragedies, including the 1899 Hurricane of San Ciriaco, the Great Fire of 1906, an earthquake in 1918, and finally the 1937 'Ponce Massacre,' in which 17 followers of Nationalist leader Pedro Albizu Campos were shot to death by police.

After World War II, Ponce began a slow economic decline. The city hit bottom in the mid-1980s, following the bankruptcy of a petrochemical complex in nearby Guayanilla and the closure of dozens of factories. In 1986, Governor Rafael Hernández Colón – himself a *ponceño* – decided enough was enough. He initiated the $450 million *Ponce en Marcha* program, a massive beautification effort that included the burying of unsightly phone and electric cables, the repaving of streets, and the renovation of nearly all structures in the downtown district. These days, Ponce is looking good.

Start at the Hotel Meliá, turn right onto Calle Cristina and left at the first intersection, Calle Mayor. Across the street is the stately

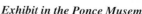
Exhibit in the Ponce Musem

Teatro La Perla, built in 1864 but partially destroyed in the 1918 earthquake. For years it was the center of Ponce social life; today, it is the home of Ponce's annual Luis Torres Nadal Theater Festival.

At the next corner is Calle Isabel and, to the right, the **Museo de la Historia de Ponce** (weekdays except Tuesday 10am–5pm; Saturday 10am–8.30pm and Sunday 11.30am–7pm). This is considered Puerto Rico's best civic museum. In fact, two hours in this place and you'll emerge an expert on all aspects of Ponce's history: geographic, economic, political, racial, medical, educational and industrial – though 45 minutes to an hour is probably sufficient.

The museum is housed in the former residence and office of Dr Guillermo Salazar Palau. It was inaugurated on December 12, 1992, on the 300th anniversary of the founding of Ponce. Admission for adults is $3, senior citizens $2, children and students $1 (includes guided tour in English or Spanish).

Start with the Ecology Room, which features a topographical map of the Ponce area, original photos of the city's development, and an exhibit on Ponce's African, Indian and European roots. The Politics Room features photos of the three Puerto Rican governors who came from Ponce: Roberto Sánchez Vilella, Luis A Ferré and Rafael Hernández Colón.

Calle Isabel

Don't miss the Architecture Room, highlighted by a huge modern glass map of the Ponce city grid, or the Health Room, which features obsolete medical instruments from the office of Dr Manuel de la Pila Iglesias, who was responsible, in 1942, for establishing Puerto Rico's first medical plan.

Outside is a 1,500-lb (680-kg) marble bathtub personally crafted in 1859 by Samuel F B Morse, inventor of the telegraph, and a brass bell donated by the crew of the warship *USS Ponce*. Walk through a passage to the adjacent Zapater residence, for exhibitions that change every six months. Here, you'll also find the huge neon sign that hung outside the Ponce office of *El Día* newspaper (forerunner of today's *El Nuevo Dia*).

As you leave the museum, turn right on **Calle Isabel**. Walk towards Calle Lolita Tizol, enjoying two blocks of Ponce's best architecture; houses here are built in the neoclassical, town creole and Spanish colonial styles, among others. This street is also the home of a popular street festival, the Fiestas de la Calle Isabel, held the third Sunday of every month.

At the end of the street is an ornate bridge, the **Puente de los Léones**. Look up at 'El León Joven' (the young lion), which symbolizes Ponce's future, then walk across to 'El León Sabio' (the wise lion), which recalls Ponce's rich and prosperous past.

Backtrack to the **Parque Tricentenario**, which – like the Ponce history museum – was

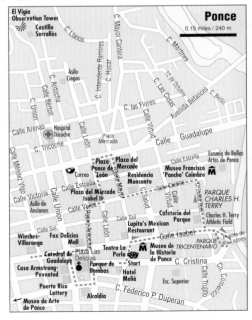

inaugurated on the city's 300th anniversary in 1992. Here you'll find a rotunda dedicated to Ponce-born architect Francisco Porrata Doria, as well as the Parque de los Ponceños Ilustres, which honors some of Ponce's outstanding citizens with medallions set among beautiful flamboyant trees.

Before leaving Tricentennial Park, note the Parque de los Próceres Latinoamericanos, which pays homage to four distinguished Latins: Venezuela's Simón Bolívar; Cuba's José Martí; the Dominican Republic's Juan Pablo Duarte, and Puerto Rico's own Luis Muñoz Marín. Also on the park's grounds are smaller monuments to former governors Luis Ferré and Rafael Hernández Colón.

Continue up **Calle Montaner**, noting the Ponce civic-pride motto on your left, hidden among the banana trees. Soon you'll see a small statue, also on your left, marking the start of **Calle Lolita Tizol**. A local violinist who died in 1933, Lolita Tizol devoted much of her life to teaching music to the children of Ponce.

Enjoying a break

If you're thirsty, buy a cold Snapple for 75 cents at the traditional **Cafeteria del Parque**, ahead on your left. The eatery also sells delicious snacks such as *empanada de queso* (cheese tortillas) for 50 cents. If you come during the week, this place is likely to be packed at lunchtime with uniformed schoolchildren from the nearby Escuela Dr Rafael Pujals. Across the street, behind a high wall, is the **Charles H Terry Athletic Field**, used as a training-ground for Spanish troops in the 1800s and later by the US military. It is dedicated to Charles H Terry, headmaster of Ponce High School early this century.

Continuing on Lolita Tizol, pass Calle Sol on your left and watch for the 'Café de Willie' sign. Here, cross Calle Montaner to the **Museo Francisco 'Pancho' Coimbre** (Tuesday to Sunday, 8am–4.30pm, free admission). This place, also known as the Ponce Sports Hall of Fame, is dedicated to favorite son Francisco Coimbre, who played baseball for the Ponce Lions from 1938 to the early 1970s. Pancho's bat is on display here, as are photos, trophies, newspaper clippings and even autographed baseballs hanging from the ceiling with invisible fishing wire. Ask any of the bilingual guides to show you around. (In addition to baseball, this is also an ideal place to use the bathrooms, which are clean and spacious, and done up in 1930s art deco style.)

The large pink building to the immediate right of the Pancho museum is the **Escuela de Bellas Artes de Ponce** (School of Fine

Art nouveau Monsanto House

Arts). A plaque on the foyer says it was constructed in 1849 as a military barracks for Spanish troops, and restored and inaugurated as a Department of Education facility in 1992. During school hours, the guard may not let you in; still, the view from outside is very impressive.

From here, make a left onto **Calle Castillo**, which – like Calle Isabel – contains many examples of Ponce's finest architectural styles. The houses range from the fancy (Nos 14 and 18) to the simple (No 22). Cross Calle Virtud and have a look at the mansion at No 34. This house, known as **Residencia Monsanto**, was built in 1913 by Federico Font and Providencia Ubides, and designed by Blas C Silva, who also designed the doctor's house we visited earlier. It is considered one of Ponce's greatest residences. As the woman of the house, Rosita Monsanto, will gladly show any visitor, it boasts the neoclassic curves of the art nouveau style and its traditional balcony and veranda is divided in two.

Cross Calle Salud, and at the next street, unmarked **Calle Mayor**, make a right. Unlike the quiet houses of Calle Castillo, this is a very commercial street, with music shops blaring the latest *merengue* hits and various pawn shops competing for customers' attention. Walk one block to Calle Estrella. The large, modern building ahead of you on your right is the **Plaza del Mercado**, a multi-story, air-conditioned produce market.

You may find many surprises here. In addition to fruit, vegetables and meats, one can shop for cheap souvenirs, lottery tickets and unusual items like coconuts and cactus rinds. There's also a natural-juice stall, 'Vuelve A Lo Natural' (Back to Nature), run by Carmen del Valle. A glass of fresh-squeezed orange, apple, lemon, grapefruit, pineapple, tamarindo, acerola, guanabana or even sesame juice is highly recommended. On the upper level of Plaza del Mercado, via escalator, are seamstress shops and at least half a dozen stores specializing in *santería* – a mixture of African voodoo and Catholicism widely practiced throughout the Caribbean. At one shop, the Botanica Marielli, you can buy 'Lady Luck Incense,' 'St Jude Spray' and even 'Seven Powers Floor Wash.'

Exit the Plaza del Mercado and cross the street into the **Plaza Ponce de León**. It's easy to miss this entrance, so look carefully for the 1926 grillwork and the beautiful tile design. Also known as Plaza de los Perros, this market was built by

Plaza de los Perros market

architect Rafael Carmoega and features Tuscan-style columns along the main gallery. It's a good place for buying cheap musical instruments, potted plants and bright plastic toys.

Come out on **Calle León**, cross the street and make a left. The long white art deco building on your right, on the other side, is the **Plaza del Mercado Isabel II**; note the black enamel tiles running along its base and the high iron ceiling, which you can glimpse through the windows. It was built in 1863, remodeled in 1903, 1938 and again in 1984, but is currently closed.

At Calle Castillo (look for the garish blue-and-yellow Pitusa sign – you can't miss it), make a right, then an immediate left onto **Paseo Atocha**. This was and still is Ponce's main commercial street, and is usually jammed with shoppers during the day. Converted into a pedestrian mall in 1990, Atocha has been beautified with trees, park benches, gaslights, silver fire hydrants and public telephones hidden in stylish black booths.

Despite its new elegance, it is still crowded with sidewalk vendors selling T-shirts, and knick-knacks of all sorts. US-owned shoe stores seem to dominate here (Payless, Foot Locker, Thom McAn), though Atocha has its share of locally-owned department stores like González Padín and Yazmín.

At Calle Isabel, the pedestrian mall ends, opening onto **Plaza Las Delicias**, Ponce's main square. Turn right and go into **Fox Delicias Mall**. A functioning movie theater from 1931 until 1980, this building has recently been transformed into a fanciful shopping and eating emporium.

On your left as you enter is a small **tourist information center**, with free maps, pamphlets and the latest issue of *Qué Pasa*. The mall is also an excellent stop for lunch. You can choose from more than a dozen fast-food outlets (Taco Maker, Pizza Hut, King Fry Chicken, Tropical Deli), or opt for more local food. If that's your preference, check out **El Bodegón**. Here, you can order *pollo al horno* (baked chicken) with rice, beans and fried banana; or you can try *pastellón de carne res* (beef stew) with, say, a side order of

Plaza Las Delicias

yucca and onion. Upstairs are boutiques and record shops; this mall even has a place for renewing drivers' licenses.

On your way out of the mall, directly ahead of you in the plaza, is a large statue of Puerto Rican autonomist **Luis Muñoz Rivera**, built in 1916 – the year of his death. If architecture fascinates you – and you don't mind the detour – make a right and pass the Pitusa sign, then walk two blocks to Calle Méndez Vigo and catch a glimpse of the huge **Wiechers-Villaronga residence**. Built in 1912, this is the finest example of neoclassical design in Ponce – and a much larger version of the Monsanto residence on Calle Cristina. Locals say it was even more beautiful before architectural renovation began in the early 1990s. There are plans to turn it into an architectural museum.

Return to the plaza and make a right. The ornate building directly across from the cathedral (and immediately before the Burger King), is the **Casa Armstrong-Poventud**. This 1899 structure serves as regional headquarters for both the Institute of Puerto Rican Culture and the Puerto Rico Tourism Company. Enter through the iron gate marked 'Librería' and check out the interior courtyard. The house also has a very small museum with Spanish artifacts and some period pieces, but it hardly compares with the history museum.

The **Catedral de Nuestra Señora de Guadalupe,** directly in front of you, traces its origin to 1670, when a group of Spanish settlers built a small church and dedicated it to the Virgin of Guadeloupe. The town of Ponce went up around this church, which was replaced in 1836. December 12 is celebrated in Ponce as the Lady of Guadeloupe Day and commemorates the city's founding. If you do this tour on weekends, you might catch the afternoon Mass at 4pm. (During the week, Mass is held at 7am, 9am and 12.05pm.) If the main entrance is closed, try the side entrance; it's almost always open.

The grayish building after the Casa Armstrong-Poventud (and the Burger King) is the **Puerto Rico Lottery**, whose tickets are hawked by vendors all over town. You're now in front of Moscoso Pharmacy, a chain founded by one of Puerto Rico's most illustrious families in 1898. Immediately to the left is the **Alcaldía** (City Hall) built in 1847.

From here, free horse-and-buggy rides around the plaza are available. Continue along this street to the end, where you will see two banks: Banco Popular de Puerto Rico and Banco Santander. The pedestrian walkway between the two is the **Paseo Antonio S Arias Ventura**, which has several sidewalk cafes and a nice evening ambience. Note the brass night-deposit safe at street level. There are very few of them left on the island, most of them having been replaced by automatic teller machines.

The whimsical Parque de Bombas

Not quite half a block directly to your left, across from Calle Cristina, is the **Parque de Bombas** – a whimsical red-and-black wooden structure built in 1882 and put into use as a firehouse the following year. Restored to its original glory in 1990, the firehouse has come to symbolize Ponce itself, and is perhaps the most-photographed building in all of Puerto Rico. Few people know that the firehouse was one of two structures built in Arabic architectural style for the 1882 Exposition. The other, known as the Kiosco Arabe, was destroyed in 1914, though a glassed-in scale model of it can be viewed in the Industry Room at the Ponce History Museum. The antique fire trucks are always a popular tourist draw. For more information on the Great Fire of 1906 and a look at firefighting techniques of the late 19th century, have a peek at the upstairs museum (daily 9.30am–5.45pm, free admission).

You are now back where you started – at the beginning of Calle Cristina – and your walking tour is over. Yet there's one more place absolutely worth seeing: the **Serrallés Castle** (Tuesday to Thursday 9:30am–4pm, Friday to Sunday 10am–5pm). A taxi to this imposing castle costs only about $3 and is highly recommended, since getting there on your own is very confusing. The easiest way to hail a cab is to walk diagonally across the plaza, past a huge statue of composer A Juan Morel Campos (father of the Puerto Rican *danza*) and the large Lion's Fountain towards Moscoso Pharmacy. Continue on Calle Concordia for about two blocks, just past Calle Luna, and watch for the taxi stands.

If you wish to drive there yourself, follow these instructions: head east on Calle Cristina past the Meliá, make a left at Calle Salud, another left at Calle Isabel, and a right at Calle León, going up the hill through some of Ponce's poorer neighborhoods. Look for the 'Malgor & Co' building on your right. At that intersection, turn left. This is Calle Guadalupe (unmarked). Make a right on Calle Bértoli, and follow signs to the Castillo Serrallés.

As you climb this curving road, you'll notice the houses getting progressively fancier and fancier. Suddenly out of nowhere you'll see **El Vigía Observation Tower** in the shape of a huge cross overlooking the city. Continue along the same street, and the Serrallés castle will soon appear on the right side. The whole trip takes 10 minutes and is exactly 1½ miles (3km).

Bilingual tours of the castle are given every half hour and last for 50 minutes. They include a 15-minute introductory film which traces the history of Don Juan Serrallés, whose family became rich and powerful during the rum and sugar boom years of the early 20th century.

A palatial Serrallés bedroom

The castle itself was designed by architect Don Pedro Adolfo de Castro y Besosa, in the 'Spanish revival' style popular throughout the United States in the 1930s. The Serrallés family moved in around 1934 and stayed until 1979. In 1986, the city of Ponce bought the castle from the estate for $500,000 – an unbelievable bargain – and spent the next three years restoring it in painstaking detail.

Among the castle's highlights are: a formal dining room with the table set for 12; a vestibule decorated with furniture of the era; an 1865 rum-distilling unit in the central interior patio, and an octagonal fountain with tiles imported from Spain. Even the kitchen is preserved with its original stove and refrigerator made of metal and porcelain. An upstairs terrace offers a spectacular view of Ponce and the Caribbean Sea.

Return to downtown Ponce in the reverse order you came, with minor variations; it's difficult to get lost getting back. If you need a taxi, tel: 842 3370 or 843 6000 from the Serrallés castle and a cab will take you back downtown for around $4.

By now, starvation is probably setting in. If seafood is your desire, take a taxi to the **Playa Ponce** area, where several excellent restaurants await you, among them: Canda's Restaurant (No 28 Calle Comercio); Restaurant El Ancla (Avenida Hostos Final No 109), or Pito's Seafood Café (Highway 2, Km 218, Las Cucharas).

If you'd rather stay in the downtown area, walk to Lupita's Mexican Restaurant at 60 Calle Isabel, where you can enjoy a chicken

or beef *chimichanga* (deep-fried tortilla topped with sour cream); *camarones Cancún* (flaming shrimps with red onion, tomato, pepper, Mexican rice, guacamole and refried beans) or Lupita's special *fajitas* for two.

Lupita's Mexican Restaurant

A guided tour of Puerto Rico's best art museum, the Museo de Arte de Ponce, considered the most sophisticated of its kind in the Caribbean.

From downtown Ponce, follow Calle Comercio (Route 133) over a new bridge that crosses the Río Portugues. Up ahead on your left is Ponce's most famous natural landmark – an ancient **ceiba tree**. The tree, surrounded by an attractive circular fence and a quiet little park, was already 50 years old when Columbus discovered the New World in 1492.

Stay on Comercio until you see the **Cafe 4 Calles** on your right side. Make a right turn here, getting on the expressway which soon becomes Avenida Las Américas. On the right is your final destination: the **Museo de Arte de Ponce** (daily 10am–5pm). There is a reasonable admission charge to the museum with reductions for children and students with ID. This is a long, low-slung modern building designed by American architect Edward Durrell Stone and completed in 1965.

The art museum's double staircase

The museum was conceived in the late 1950s by Governor Luis A Ferré, founder of the New Progressive Party. It started with 71 paintings; today it has more than 1,800 registered works. On a marble plaque at the entrance, Ferré says the museum's purpose is 'to broaden the understanding of our own and other cultures through the contact with and appreciation of the visual arts, thus to enhance the quality of life in Puerto Rico.'

To appreciate the museum fully, try to visit its galleries in chronological order. The best way is to start in the lobby surrounding the museum's trademark double staircase. Here are the oldest paintings in the collection, 14th-century works such as *Madonna and Child* by Luca di Tommé, *A Hebrew Prophet* by Giovanni del Biondo, and Leandro Rosanno's 16th-century masterpiece, *The Flood*.

Go upstairs and continue with the **Spanish School** gallery. Here you'll find Alonso Sánchez Coello's *Lady With a Pink*, and two works by José de Ribera, *St Paul* and *St Jerome*, as well as Pedro de Mena's lifelike sculpture, *Sorrowing Virgin*. Next, pass into the **Flemish School** and enjoy Peter Paul Rubens' *The Greek Magus* and David Teniers' *The Temptation of St Anthony*.

Then come three galleries dedicated to Italian art. The first is the **Northern Italian School** (Giovanni Battista Langetti's *The Torture of Ixion*), the **Florence and Bologna Schools** (Ludovico Cigola's *St Francis of Assisi*) and the **Rome and Naples Schools** (*Antiochus*

Northern Italian gallery

and Stratonice by Pompeo Girolamo Batoni). From here, visit the **Dutch School** gallery, which contains Peter Verelst's *The Philosopher* and the *Vanitas* still life by Pieter Roestraeten (1678). The last gallery on this floor is the **French School**, containing, among other works, *The Origin of Painting* by Louis-Jean-François Cagrene, and *Greek Lady at the Bath* by Joseph Marie Vien.

Come back downstairs, passing the gift shop on your left. On either side of you, along the hallways, are French paintings from the 19th century and German paintings through the ages (including the frightening *Judith with the Head of Holofernes* by Lucas Cranach). Turn left into the **British School** gallery. Here, behind glass, is Sir Frederick Leighton's *Flaming June*, completed in 1895, the year before his death. This painting has become a symbol of the museum itself. Above it hangs *Sleeping Beauty* by Sir Edward Burne-

Jones, and covering the entire far wall, is the Burne-Jones' masterpiece, *The Sleep of King Arthur in Avalon*.

Also in this wonderful gallery are *The School of Nature* by William Holman Hunt, and Benjamin West's *Resurrection of Christ*. In the last room on this wing are several Russian paintings, the most famous being Konstantin Jegorovitch Makovski's *The Choosing of the Bride*.

The two final galleries on the other side of the lobby are dedicated to the **Puerto Rican School**. Here, as a fitting way to end the tour, is a delightful reminder of the landmark where we started the morning: Francisco Oller's watercolor, *The Ceiba of Ponce*.

Giovanni Bologna's 'Neptune'

A visit to the Tibes Indian Ceremonial Park, with its ancient burial ground and museum. After lunch, visit Cerro de Punta – the island's highest peak – and Cerro Maravilla, site of a major political scandal in the late 1970s, then continue on to the Toro Negro Forest Reserve and the Doña Juana waterfall. Try to be on the road by 9am and note that Tibes is closed on Monday.

Leave Ponce by taking one-way **Calle Cristina** out of the downtown district, passing Ponce High School on your right. Follow the curve and go over the **Puente de los Leónes** (Lions' Bridge). Continue about a quarter of a mile and make a left on Highway 14, also known as Avenída Fagot. Follow easily legible signs to the **Tibes Indian Ceremonial Park**, passing through some of Ponce's nicest residential suburbs. At the T-junction, make a left, then another left at La Llave Mini-Market. On your right are some spectacular modern mansions. If the gate is open, drive up the hill and have a peek. Come back down and make a right, continuing along this very pleasant country road.

You'll soon cross a narrow, one-lane bridge. At the stop sign, turn left and go down the hill to the antique 'Corona' sign at the roadside bar. Corona, once Puerto Rico's most famous beer, was driven out of business in the mid-1980s by competition from US brands. At the Esso station (in the States, Esso long ago became Exxon), make a right onto Route 503. Tibes will be on your right-hand side, at Km 2.7. From downtown Ponce, the trip should take 15 to 25 minutes, depending on traffic. There is a small admission charge to the park (Tuesday to Sunday, 9am–

Severed heads

4pm) with reductions for students and children and it includes a 30-minute guided tour in English or Spanish; due to vandalism and litter problems, visitors are no longer allowed to wander around the grounds alone.

'Tibes' – an indigenous name for 'rough stone' – consists of seven courts, two ceremonial areas, burial sites and numerous artifacts. The complex was discovered by a farmer in 1975 after Hurricane Eloise hit the island, uncovering previously hidden rock formations. The local archaeological society followed up with an extensive study, after which the city of Ponce expropriated 32 acres (13ha) and established the Tibes Indian Ceremonial Park in 1982.

The site is believed to have been inhabited by the Igneris, who lived in Puerto Rico between 100 and 700AD, and the pre-Taínos, who followed them. The Igneris were farmers who made pottery and began the concept of the 'cemi,' or deformed skulls. They used bows and arrows, inhaled drugs and slept in hammocks – customs later

Green vista on the Ruta Panoramica

adapted by the Taínos, about 50,000 of whom inhabited the island when Columbus arrived in 1493. A professional guide will escort you over a footbridge and through a garden of Indian medicinal plants and trees, including the rare *moralón* – of which only 15 are known to exist. The area is dotted with *higuera* trees, noted for their bright-green leaves. At Yucayeque, a recreated Indian village, you can see how the Igneris and pre-Taínos lived in *bateyes* or thatched-roof huts.

Nearby, at the Tibes cemetery, archaeologists have found some 130 skeletal remains, including some of those believed to have been the victims of human sacrifice. The petroglyphs or rock drawings are hard to discern (the ones outside Utuado are much better), though exhibits at the park's museum do an excellent job of explaining it all.

Leaving Tibes, make a right back onto Route 503, which soon begins to climb. Within 10 miles (16km), the winding two-lane road improves a little and gives way to awesome views of the Caribbean. At Route 143 – the Ruta Panorámica – make a right turn, following the arrow to Barranquitas.

This road, one of several that form the **Panoramic Route** from Mayagüez to Yabucoa, follows the backbone of the Cordillera Central and wends its way through some of Puerto Rico's most breathtaking scenery. Ferns, bamboo trees and *impatiens* line the two-lane blacktop, which offers new vistas of mountains and greenery with every hairpin turn of the road. On your right, at the intersection with

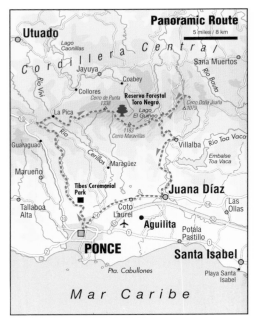

Satisfied customers

Route 140, is the restaurant **Lechonera La Pica**. (This easy-to-miss place is closed, unfortunately, on Monday, Tuesday and Wednesday – on these days it's advisable to pack your own lunch.) La Pica, owned by Carmen López, is an ideal stop to enjoy the views as well as a cheap and good local *cordillera* cuisine. Try the house specialty, *lechón con arroz y habichuelas* (roast pork with rice and beans) for only about $3 – or *arroz con pollo* (barbecue chicken with rice and pigeon peas). You can also order inexpensive fried snacks such as *mofongo* (plantains filled with bacon bits) or *empanadilla de cerdo o pollo* (chicken or pork fritters).

After lunch and an inspection of the owner's impressive collection of antique bottles and farming implements, continue on Route 143 to **Cerro de Punta**, at 4,390ft (1,338m) the island's highest mountain. From its summit, one can see both the Atlantic Ocean and the Caribbean Sea. An unmarked gravel road goes up to the peak, but don't even think about driving up; only official four-wheel-drive vehicles are permitted. Even if you're tempted at first, one look at its steepness will probably make you change your mind.

Cerro Maravilla, about 5 miles (8km) down the road, isn't as high (3,880ft/1,183m) but is far more accessible – and it occupies a very important place in recent Puerto Rican history. On July 25, 1978, two young independence supporters planning to blow up the WRIK-TV transmitting tower atop the mountain were killed by policemen who had been tipped off about the plan. The deaths triggered an investigation, which soon revealed a cover-up by Puerto Rico's pro-statehood governor at the time, Carlos Romero Barceló. A major scandal ensued, costing Romero Barceló his bid for re-election, turning the young men into martyrs and damaging the credibility of the statehood party for years afterward. The scandal produced numerous books, among them *Requiem on Cerro Maravilla*, by Manny Suárez and Tomás Stella, and the less-than-accurate movie *Show of Force*, starring Amy Irving.

Oddly, no sign directs you to the spot where it all happened, and the gravel road you need to get there – Route 577 – doesn't even appear on the official highway map. Nevertheless, make a left at 577 and ascend the hill, passing several TV antennas. At the end of this tiny road, look carefully and you'll see two stone crosses marking the graves of the two revolutionaries murdered there – Arnaldo Dario Rosado and Carlos Soto Arriví – surrounded by flowers and Puerto Rican flags. Don't be surprised to find several people at the site; in the last decade, it has become a shrine for those who support the cause of Puerto Rican independence.

Return to Route 143. Across from Cerro Maravilla on the right side is a pleasant picnic area with brick tables and benches. Further up the road is **Lago El Guineo**, a pristine mountain lake hidden at the end of an unmarked gravel road that takes a bit of finding. Look for a small wooden sign on the left that says 'Prohibido Tirar Basura – D R N' (Don't dump garbage). Take that road to the end, past a private house, a basketball hoop and a junked car of unknown vintage. Park and hike down this very steep and slippery path. The 10-minute walk is well worth it: a beautiful lake shrouded in mist, its stillness broken only by the sounds of ducks and *coquí* frogs.

Continue on Route 143, following the signs to Ciales. Keep left as you enter the **Reserva Forestal Toro Negro**, which is part of the US Caribbean National Forest. For a nice 10-minute detour, stay on 143 until you reach the 200-ft (61-m) high **Doña Juana waterfall**. Return to the forest's entrance and pick up Route 149, following the signs to Villalba. Soon you'll see the **Embalse Toa Vaca**, one of Puerto Rico's largest dams, appear on your left side, with the Caribbean shimmering in the distance.

Villalba, to your left, was one of the first places in Puerto Rico to get electricity, telephones and modern toilets. Today, this mountain town of 25,000

Doña Juana falls

boasts several interesting factories – including a Westinghouse plant that produces computer chips and a Medtronic facility where workers assemble components for heart pacemakers.

At the town of **Juana Díaz** – known for its excellence in producing *mavi*, a local fruit drink – turn right onto Highway 14. This quickly brings you to **Coto Laurel**, home to Puerto Rico's largest mango exporter, Fruits International. Company president Ehud Peikes, a native of Israel, will be happy to show you around his 100,000-tree orchard. To get there, make a right turn at Route 511 and drive ¾ mile (1km), at which point you'll find a dirt road leading directly to the Pango Mango packing-house on your right.

Return to Highway 14, which, upon entering Ponce, becomes

Avenida Tito Castro. Make a left turn at the big Plaza del Mercado (Calle Mayor). This will bring you directly back to the center of town, where you started.

Ehud Peikes, mango exporter

12. West from Ponce

Driving west from Ponce, visit historic San Germán on the way to Cabo Rojo National Wildlife Preserve, the Cabo Rojo lighthouse and Playa Boquerón. Dinner and/or overnight stop at La Parguera; return to Ponce next morning.

Leave Ponce via Highway 2, passing the modern Plaza del Caribe shopping mall on your left. Once you spot the Holiday Inn on a hill overlooking the sea, you know you've left the big city and are on your way to Puerto Rico's scenic southwestern region.

About 10 miles (16km) west of Ponce is the sprawling Peñuelas petrochemical complex, built in the heady days before the 1973–4 Arab oil embargo. The rusting refinery now sits idle by the roadside, its US owners bankrupt and its shell an embarrassing eyesore. Further west, the superhighway skirts three interesting towns: **Guayanilla**, believed to be the home of Agüeybaná, *cacique* or chief of Puerto Rico's long-extinct Taíno Indians; **Yauco**, where some of the island's best gourmet coffee is produced, and **Sabana Grande**, site of the famous Pozo del Virgen, a religious shrine that attracts thousands of devout Catholics every year.

You're now a stone's throw from Puerto Rico's second-oldest city, **San Germán**, founded in 1573 and home today to about 35,000 people. Exit the highway at Route 122 and go past the shopping mall. Upon entering town, bear right and follow the signs to **Museo Porta Coeli**, the starting point of a leisurely one-hour walking tour that takes you to San Germán's most important sites. If you can, find a nearby parking space on the long rectangular plaza at the center of town and ascend the steps of this historic church.

Porta Coeli – Latin for 'heaven's gate' – is one of the oldest Catholic shrines in the western hemisphere. It dates from 1606,

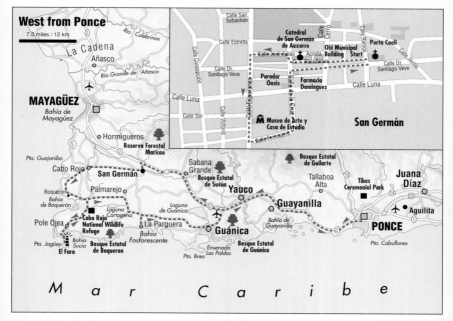

Porta Coeli church

when the island's bishop, Friar Martín Vásquez de Arce, issued a license authorizing the building of the convent. In 1866, the original convent was demolished, and its bricks and beams were sold at public auction (only the chapel and part of the convent's original front walls were left standing). Twelve years later, however, Porta Coeli was restored and opened for services. The church (daily, 9am–noon and 1–4pm, free admission) is today a small religious museum. Among its treasured possessions are two wood carvings of a black Nuestra Señora de Monserrat, one from the 18th century, one from the 19th. Also worth seeing is the carved main altar, whose niches are adorned with small wooden statues made by Puerto Rican, Spanish, Colombian and Mexican artists.

After leaving Porta Coeli, walk the length of the plaza along Calle Ruíz Belvis, which at the next corner meets Calle Cerro. On your right is the **Old Municipal Building**, a large cream-colored structure erected between 1839 and 1844. Until 1950, this building served as the town prison, among other functions; it's now being restored. Directly in front of this building is **Plaza Francisco Mariano Quiñones**, the commercial and social center of San Germán since the 19th century. The large **Catédral de San Germán de Auxerre** – built in 1739 to honor the town's French patron saint – dominates the plaza. Take a sidestreet, Calle José *San Germán man* Julián Acosta, for about a block, passing some interesting wooden dwellings, and turn left at Calle Esperanza. The **Museo de Arte y Casa de Estudio**, three blocks ahead on your left at No 7, has many paintings, both modern and classic, by local artists.

Make a left at Calle Ferrocarril, the first intersection after the museum, and another left at Calle de la Cruz, arriving back in the center of town just in time for lunch. If you're really hungry, enjoy a full-course Puerto Rican meal at the **Parador Oasis**, located at the corner of Cruz and Calle Luna, the town's main drag. If, however, all you want is a snack, try **Restaurante La Botica** – a sandwich shop recently established on the site of the old Farma-

Wild Cabo Rojo

cía Dominguez. The owner of this former apothecary, founded in 1877, has kept all the obsolete glass bottles and drugstore paraphernalia displayed on the shelves for customers to enjoy.

After lunch, retrieve your car and get on Calle Luna, which becomes Route 102 as it passes Interamerican University on your right and heads out of town. At this point, the road takes a sharp left, almost a U-turn; make sure you follow the signs to 'Lajas/Cabo Rojo' or you'll end up on Route 318 heading towards Mayagüez. Endless fields of sugar cane characterize this region, which has the flattest land anywhere in Puerto Rico.

Route 102 brings you right through the center of **Cabo Rojo**, a *municipio* of 38,000 known far more for its famous lighthouse and pristine beaches than for its decaying downtown area. Keep going straight. On the outskirts of town, make a left at Route 100, a nice modern highway, and follow it all the way to the end.

After all this driving, you may be tempted to hop over to beautiful **Boquerón** – a perfect place for suntans, beach games, oysters and ice-cold Medalla beer. But first, you should explore two very interesting places only a few miles down the road. Take Route 101 east to the hamlet of Las Arenas, then follow Route 301 south until you come to **Cabo Rojo National Wildlife Refuge** on the left (if you pass the Isla gasoline station, you've gone too far).

This peaceful wildlife preserve, (weekdays 7am–3.30pm), contains a small museum about the area's natural history. It's also the site of some very unusual experiments. One which I've actually participated in – under the auspices of the non-profit group Earthwatch – involves injecting wild mongooses with electronic transponders in order to track their movements. The long-term project seeks to study the mongooses' life cycles, and is eventually aimed at preventing the spread of rabies by these voracious little creatures, which seem to eat everything in sight.

It's only 5 miles (8km) or so from the wildlife refuge to **El Faro**, a lonely lighthouse on Puerto Rico's southwestern corner, which you can probably see from your car window, looking to the left. But the last two miles are unpaved – and that's where the fun begins. Make sure you have a full tank of gas and a strong stomach; the potholes on this dirt road will shake you up, to say the least. If the potholes prove too much, stop at **El Caracól**, a beachfront shack which serves tasty seafood meals and delicious homemade lemonade.

At the end of the dirt road, park your car and walk the last 330ft (100m) up to the lighthouse. The structure itself, built by the Spanish in 1882 and today covered with graffiti, may be something of a disappointment – especially if you've been to the beautifully restored lighthouse at Cabezas de San Juan near Fajardo. The view, however, is something else. Few spots in the world are more dramatic than this one, known as **Punta Jagüey**, where waves crash against the steep cliffs below and the shimmering Caribbean seems to surround you in every direction. On particularly clear days, you can even glimpse **Isla de Mona** – an uninhabited island sitting midway between Puerto Rico and the Dominican Republic.

If you didn't stop at Boquerón before, do so now before the mosquitoes come out and eat you alive (by that time, the public beach area will be closed anyway). Then get back on Route 101 going

east. Ahead on the right is **Laguna Cartagena**, a bird sanctuary whose tranquility was upset a few years ago when UFOs were reported in the area. For a whole summer, thousands of people descended on the shores every night. They didn't see many little green men, but they left lots of trash behind.

At the first intersection, make a right onto Route 303, then a

Caribbean surfing

left onto Route 305. Both are scenic country roads lined with old sugar mills and cow pastures. Follow 305 as it crosses Route 116, turns into Route 304 and brings you straight into **La Parguera**, a tiny fishing village that has become a major tourist resort.

At the **Parador Villa Parguera**, you can get a delicious dinner for around $20. Incidentally, the *parador* isn't a bad place to spend the night. There are numerous bars and seaside salsa clubs here and Parguera is also known for its proximity to the famous Phosphorescent Bay, whose waters are illuminated on moonless nights by billions of one-celled dinoflagellates that make up plankton.

If you need to get back to Ponce quickly, return to Route 116 and take it all the way to **Guánica**, where it merges with Highway 2. Be sure to take a right towards Yauco or you'll head the other way for miles without knowing it.

If you decide to stay overnight at La Parguera, you can return to Ponce via Route 324. This brings you to Route 116 and Guánica then on to Highway 2, which takes you straight back to Ponce.

Parguera after dark

An early-morning visit to Hacienda Buena Vista, a 19th-century coffee plantation, then on to Adjuntas, the world's largest producer of citron. After lunch, visit the Caguana Indian Ceremonial Park, then backtrack through Utuado for a relaxing dinner and overnight stay at Parador Casa Grande. Call Hacienda Buena Vista, tel: 722 5882 or 848 7020 in advance. Leave Ponce by 7.45am to join the 8.30am tour to avoid heat and crowds. Buena Vista is closed on Monday and Tuesday.

To leave downtown Ponce, drive west on Calle Isabel, which quickly becomes Calle Reina. This street goes through some very poor neighborhoods. Notice the row of bright red wooden houses off to the right as you pass **Calle 25 de Enero**, named for the January 25, 1906, fire that almost destroyed Ponce. At the end of the street (at the green sign marked 'Administración de Servicios Generales'), make a right. Go one block and turn left onto Calle Victoria. Immediately after the garish funeral home on your left is the intersection with Route 10. Follow the arrow to Adjuntas.

Looming in the distance is the Puerto Rican Cement Co, the island's largest cement producer. Soon after, Highway 10 rises into the mountains. Continue along the winding road, which unfortunately has more than its share of trash. At Km 16.8, turn left into **Hacienda Buena Vista**, a coffee plantation authentically restored to its 19th-century charm.

The farm – operated by the non-profit Conservation Trust of Puerto Rico – dates from 1833, the year nobleman Salvador de Vives bought 482 *cuerdas* of land from the Spanish government, which

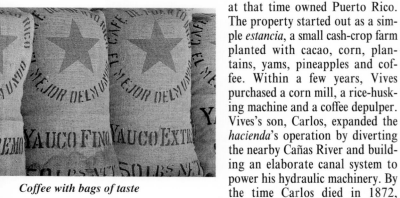

Coffee with bags of taste

at that time owned Puerto Rico. The property started out as a simple *estancia*, a small cash-crop farm planted with cacao, corn, plantains, yams, pineapples and coffee. Within a few years, Vives purchased a corn mill, a rice-husking machine and a coffee depulper. Vives's son, Carlos, expanded the *hacienda*'s operation by diverting the nearby Cañas River and building an elaborate canal system to power his hydraulic machinery. By the time Carlos died in 1872, Puerto Rican coffee had acquired the best reputation in the world. Documents from Rome show that the Vatican imported only Puerto Rican gourmet beans for the Pope's morning coffee.

The island's coffee fame, however, came to a sudden end in 1899, when Hurricane San Ciriaco destroyed 60 percent of the island's crop. The same year, international coffee prices collapsed, forcing Hacienda Buena Vista to slash production from 33,500lb (14,600kg)

Salto Vives waterfall

of coffee in 1897 to just 7,800lb (3,540kg) in 1900. In the early 20th century, Buena Vista was abandoned, and termites gradually took over the property. Much of the original machinery had been left at the site, but it was badly deteriorated and covered with rust from the tropical climate. In 1984, when the Conservation Trust took over the plantation, restorers began working at the site, using 19th-century techniques to recreate the plantation atmosphere. Today, all the machinery is intact and working, and the rooms of the manor have been restored to 1890's style, complete with furniture donated by the Vives family.

There is an admission charge to Hacienda Buena Vista, with reductions for children. The tours are conducted in Spanish, but all guides are bilingual and can answer questions in English. Tours last about two hours and include a 10-minute walk to the Salto Vives waterfall.

Leaving Hacienda Buena Vista, take a left and continue on Highway 10. You will soon come to the colorful town of **Adjuntas** (population 20,000), center of the island's coffee and banana industry. Adjuntas also produces 65 percent of the world supply of citron – an essential ingredient in fruit cakes. Immigrants from the French island of Corsica began growing citron trees in Puerto Rico more than 100 years ago, though the mysterious fruit is mentioned in the Bible and has been prized since Roman times. Today, two companies produce the bulk of the town's $2 million worth of annual citron exports. Most production goes to Holland and Germany.

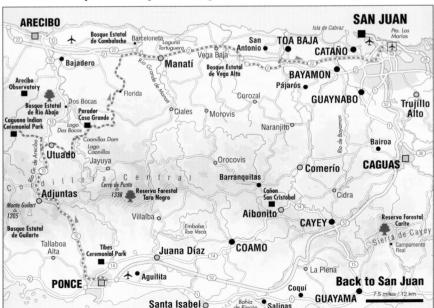

Yes, we have some bananas

If you wish you can visit a citron-processing plant in operation. Right outside town, after a couple of garment assembly factories lining Highway 10, is the first of the two: **Citron Export Inc**, which lies at the end of an unmarked path leading off from the main road. The manager, Andries DeJong, is a Dutch expatriate who has lived in Adjuntas for more than 30 years; he's always proud to receive visitors. If Mr DeJong isn't in, drop by the other citron plant, **Cooperativa Cosecheras de Cidra**, which is only half a mile (1km) out of the way. To find it, continue up the road over the tiny bridge, turn left at Route 135 and over another, even smaller, bridge. Go 450ft (140m) and on the left side, you'll see the Cooperativa sign. Follow the road all the way to the end, passing through a grove of citron trees, and ask for Vicente Martínez.

The next stop along the route is **Utuado**, a small city of 35,000 founded in 1739. In April 1986, Utuado received international press coverage after one of its native sons, Captain Salvador Ribas Dominicci, was killed in a US bombing raid over Libya (shortly thereafter, San Juan's Isla Grande airfield was renamed in memory of the young pilot). But before entering Utuado, make a left onto Route 603, following the signs toward Arecibo. Go over the bridge and continue on Highway 10. At the cemetery, turn right, and at the next traffic light, make a left onto Route 111. The **Caguana Indian Ceremonial Park** (daily, 9:30am–4:30pm) appears on the left side about 7 winding miles (11.5km) later.

Caguana is one of the most important historical sites in Puerto Rico. Built by the Taínos nearly 1,000 years ago, the ballpark includes 10 *bateyes* on which the Indians played a game similar to lacrosse. The ritual had religious as well as athletic significance. The entrance path is lined with tall stately coconut palms, leading to a small circular museum with Taíno artifacts. The Indians who inhabited Caguana were much more recent than those at Tibes; hence the much clearer petroglyphs, or rock drawings. A large ceiba tree sits at the park's center, its roots branching out in all directions, and an even larger moca tree provides shade nearby.

Fortunately, there is no charge to enter this beautifully landscaped park, but there are no tour guides to show you around.

Outside the museum, an unofficial guide may attach himself to you, offering to explain the sites for a small fee. If you don't need his services, make it clear immediately, or you may find yourself paying later.

Before departing Caguana, walk to the far end of the park and take a 10-minute hike down to the banks of the Río Tamaná. Note the proliferation of coffee trees to your right, on the other side of the fence, and the karst hills towering in the distance.

When you leave Caguana, get on Route 111 and follow the signs back to Utuado. Stay on 111 right through town and into the mountains again. At the Esso station, make a left onto Route 140. Remain on this road for the next 18 miles (29km), driving directly over the **Caonillas Dam** (built by the Puerto Rico Water Resources Authority in 1948). At the intersection with Route 613, stop for a scenic view of the dam through tall pine trees.

You could probably make it all the way back to San Juan tonight, but why push it? Better to continue another half a mile and exit at Route 612, going down the hill around a curve and over a very narrow bridge. **Parador Casa Grande** will be on your left side. Casa Grande, opened in 1988, has 20 rooms and charges approximately \$55–60 for a single or double. Dinner, served on a beautiful terrace overlooking the mountains, is around another \$12. Try the succulent *pollo guisado* (chicken stew), which comes with rice, pigeon peas, beans, *tostones* and a dessert of *guava con queso*. You've driven only 60 miles (95km) today, but it probably feels more like 600. Don't worry; the cool mountain breezes and the *coquís* will lull you to sleep. Next morning, after delicious local coffee, breakfast and a dip in the pool, leave Casa Grande by taking a right turn on Route 612 over the same bridge you came in on. At Route 140, make a left and follow it for the next 22 miles (35km), all the way to Highway 2.

The journey is an interesting ride. The road takes you through some dramatic karst country as well as the unmarked little town of **Florida**, Puerto Rico's newest municipality (founded in 1971). After Florida, Route 140 becomes a major highway.

At **Barceloneta**, note the Lotus factory off to the right. This is where most of Puerto Rico's pineapple juice is canned. Pick up Highway 22 and follow the 'Autopista' signs all the way back to San Juan.

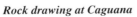

Rock drawing at Caguana

Eating Out

Puerto Rico must have a higher concentration of McDonald's, Burger Kings and KFCs than any place on earth. Almost nonexistent 15 years ago, these plastic eateries now seem to dominate every street corner in San Juan. If fast food isn't your fancy, however, Puerto Rico still offers a wide array of choices for quality dining – from sidewalk '*come y vetes*' (literally, eat-and-run joints) to extravagant restaurants with tuxedoed waiters, tropical gardens, valet parking and New York prices.

The very best places are clustered along the Condado and Isla Verde hotel strip, along Avenida F D Roosevelt in Hato Rey, and in Old San Juan. Reservations are recommended (and in some cases required) for the fancier ones, where dress tends to be on the formal side.

While in San Juan, you can eat Chinese, Japanese, Thai, Spanish, French, Italian, Mexican, Arab or American food. For authentic local cuisine, try any of the restaurants listed below under 'Puerto Rican.' Island cooking features such dishes as *arroz con pollo* (chicken with annato-colored rice and seasonings); *lechón asao* (pit-roasted pork); *pasteles* (shredded plantain, *yuca* and *yautía* patties filled with diced pork, chickpeas, hard-boiled eggs and red peppers wrapped in plantain leaves and boiled), *asopao de marisco* (fish stew) and *sancocho* (a stew made from tubers and diced meat). Some popular side dishes include *tostones* (refried green plantains); *mofongo* (plantains mashed with garlic and fried pork rinds), and *amarillos* (yellow slices of sweet plantains sautéed in butter or olive oil).

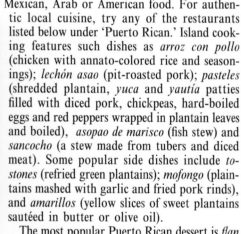

A simple meal

The most popular Puerto Rican dessert is *flan* (custard), made of cheese, coconut or vanilla. Another favorite is *guava con queso* (candied fruit slices with cheese). Either one of these should be enjoyed with a strong cup of *café puertorriqueño*, with or without milk.

Following is a list of San Juan-area restaurants worth checking out. For dining spots outside the metro area, consult the latest issue of *Qué Pasa*, published quarterly by the Puerto Rico Tourism Company. Guide to restaurant prices: **$** = average entrée under $10; **$$** = average entrée $10–20; **$$$** = average entrée over $20.

American

DUNBAR'S
1954 McLeary, Ocean Park
Tel: 728 2920
Favorite *gringo* hangout; buffalo chicken wings and dart games. $

EL HAMBURGER
402 Muñoz Rivera, Puerta de Tierra
Tel: 725 5891
Rustic eatery overlooking the Atlantic. Enjoy the best flame-broiled burgers in town. $

HARD ROCK CAFÉ
253 Recinto Sur, Old San Juan
Tel: 724 7625
Musical memorabilia and delicious food (try the 'veggie burger'). $

HOOTERS
413 San Francisco, Old San Juan
Tel: 722-9464
Famous chicken wings, seafood, sandwiches and snacks. $

Arab

JERUSALEM RESTAURANT
O'Neill I-6, Hato Rey
Tel: 764 3265
Palestinian owners offer Arab delights such as grilled leg of lamb, stuffed grape leaves and cardamom coffee. $$

MIDDLE EAST RESTAURANT
207 Padre Colón, Río Piedras
Tel: 751 7304
Traditional Arab food; belly-dancing on weekends. $$

Caribbean

MANGO'S CAFÉ
2421 Laurel, Punta Las Marias
Tel: 727-9328
Jamaican, West Indian and Creole food, drinks and music. $

Thirst-quenching fruit

TROPICAL
Borinquen Towers I, Caparra Heights
Tel: 781 1528
Cuban restaurant. Everything from *arroz con pollo* to stuffed Cornish hen with *congri*. $$

French

C'EST LA VIE
Ashford and Magdalena, Condado
Tel: 721 6075
Crêpes, *fajitas*, sirloin burgers. $$

CHALET 313
313 Recinto Sur, Old San Juan
Fresh seafood, rack of lamb, filet mignon, paella and pastries. $$$

LA CHAUMIERE
367 Tetuán, Old San Juan
Tel: 722 3330
Dishes include scallopine of veal with medallion of lobster, asparagus and Béarnaise sauce. Reserve. $$$

Italian

CARUSO RESTAURANT
1104 Ashford, Condado
Classic Italian cuisine featuring ten-

Sizzling on the charcoal

der baby veal, colossal shrimp, home-made lasagna and flaming desserts. $

Via Appia
1350 Ashford, Condado
Tel: 725 8711
Sidewalk cafe featuring pizza and basic pasta dishes. $

La Scala
Ambassador Plaza Hotel, Condado
Northern Italian cuisine in a modern, elegant setting; specialities include *gnocchi*, *tortellini* and black pasta. $$$

Mexican

Amanda's
424 Norzagaray, Old San Juan
Tel: 722 1682
Nice for drinks and ocean view, but French-Mexican dishes and vegetable plates are overpriced. Slow service. $$

Pancho's
1350 Ashford, Condado
Tel: 725-5511
Mexican specialities served on a terrace fronting busy Ashford Avenue. $

Lupi's
Route 187, Km 1.3, Isla Verde
Tel: 253 2198
Mexican bar with an American flavor. Delicious *fajitas* and flying fish, and best *margaritas* in San Juan. $

Maria's
202 Cristo, Old San Juan
Nice bar, but Mexican-style food tastes like plastic and 'tropical drinks' are mostly artificial. $

Oriental

Back Street Hong Kong
El San Juan Hotel
Tel: 791 1224
In a pagoda used as the Hong Kong Pavilion in the 1962 New York World's Fair. Mandarin, Szechuan and Hunan dishes. Reservations. $$$

Lotus Flower
Condado Plaza Hotel
Tel: 722 0940
One of the best restaurants in Puerto Rico. Szechuan, Hunan, Mandarin, Cantonese cuisine. Reservations. $$$

Yukiyu
311 Recinto Sur, Old San Juan
Tel: 721 0653
Japanese Teppan-yaki restaurant and sushi lover's paradise. $$$

Traditional seafood at Amadeus

Puerto Rican

Ajili Mojili
Joffre and Clemenceau streets, Condado. Tel: 725-9195
Authentic native dishes with a gourmet twist. $$$

Amadeus
106 San Sebastián, Old San Juan
Tel: 722 8635
Traditional Puerto Rican dinners, fresh seafood. Delicious *ceviche*. $$

CASITA BLANCA
351 Tapia, Santurce
Tel: 726 5501
Outstanding local cuisine in cafe restaurant, but located in one of Santurce's worst neighborhoods. Has been mentioned in *Gourmet* magazine and *The New York Times.* **$**

LA BOMBONERA
259 San Francisco, Old San Juan
Tel: 722 0658
The best place in Old San Juan for a cheap, satisfying *arroz con pollo* and coffee with local pastry. **$**

LA MALLORQUINA
207 San Justo, Old San Juan
Tel: 722 3261
Oldest restaurant in Puerto Rico; specialties are *asopao de marisco* and *arroz con pollo*. Worth a visit for interior courtyard alone. Reservations. **$$**

Spanish

COMPOSTELA
106 Av Condado
Tel: 724 6088
Rated excellent by *San Juan City Magazine*, which recommends royal pheasant with raspberry sauce. **$$$**

LA CASONA
609 San Jorge esq Fernández Juncos, Santurce
Tel: 727 2717
Expensive restaurant in old Spanish-style home replete with tropical gardens. Lobster salad, stuffed rabbit loin and the best *paella* in Puerto Rico. Reservations. **$$$**

LA ZARAGOZANA
356 San Francisco, Old San Juan
Tel: 723 5103
Fancy Spanish restaurant featuring dishes like filet of pork and *pollo andaluza*. Big bucks, slow service. **$$$**

Steak and Seafood

AUGUSTO'S CUISINE
Hotel Excelsior, Miramar
Tel: 725-7700
Winner of the prestigious Golden Fork Award for four consecutive years. **$$$**

CHART HOUSE
1214 Ashford, Condado
Tel: 728 0110
Fresh seafood, prime-rib restaurant with verandas. **$$$**

DAR TIFFANY
El San Juan Hotel, Isla Verde
Tel: 791 7272
Award-winning restaurant. Dry-aged prime beef, Maine lobster. **$$$**

LA CASITA
27 Manuel Enrique, Cataño
Tel: 788 5080
Fancy restaurant in a poor neighborhood; delicious fresh fish including octopus cocktail. **$$$**

MARISQUERIA ATLANTICA
7 Lugo Vinas, Puerta de Tierra
Tel: 722 0890
The Atlantica prides itself on being 'friendliest fresh food and fish restaurant in town.'

Vegetarian

CAFÉ BERLIN
407 San Francisco, Old San Juan
Tel: 722 5205
Fresh pastas, organic foods and delicious salad bar. Portions slightly on the small side. **$$**

A choice of refreshment

Calendar of Special Events

JANUARY – APRIL

Three Kings' Day (Los Tres Reyes), Puerto Rico's traditional gift-giving day, falls on January 6th, Epiphany. Islandwide festivals feature music, dancing, parades and feasts, with a display of the Three Wise Men on their camels at the entrance to Old San Juan.

The Areyto is the focus of the **International Folklore Festival**, and the outdoor **Fiesta de San Sebastian**, held January 19–21, attracts artists, musicians and spectators to Old San Juan.

In February, the **Coffee Harvest Festival** in Maricao, which celebrates one of Puerto Rico's oldest exports, features folk music, parades, authentic cuisine and a demonstration of coffee-preparation techniques. Later in the month is **Carnival**; Ponce is known for especially lively celebrations.

In March, another Ponce event, the **Regional Crafts Fair**, features native arts and crafts, while the two-day **Feria Dulce Sueño** in Guayama is dedicated to the exhibition of fine horses and Cinco Días con Nuestra Tierra is an agro-industrial fair in Mayaguez.

In April, San Germán holds its **sugar harvest festival**, while three south coast towns – Guayama, Salinas and Juana Díaz – celebrate their patron saint festivals. The **Maví Carnival** in Juana Díaz honors the town's uniquely flavored maví beverage.

MAY – AUGUST

The week-long **Semana de la Danza** recognizes one of Puerto Rico's national dance forms, the *danza*, in an Old San Juan program that includes dances, recitals, choral concerts and other competitions. Weaving, *mundillo* lace, native dishes and music are the focus of the **Puerto Rican Weaving Festival**, held in Isabela. Over the long Memorial Day weekends Old San

February carnival in Ponce

Festival-goers in San Sebastián

Juan bops to the **Heineken Jazz Fest**, featuring big names in Latin jazz.

June is filled with special events, including Ponce's Afro-Caribbean **Bomba y Plena Festival** and the world-renowned **Casals Festival**, an international competition started by Spanish cellist Pablo Casals. Then comes **San Juan Bautista Day** on the 24th, when *sanjuaneros* walk backwards into the sea three times at midnight for good luck. Towards the month's end is the **Aibonito Flower Festival**.

In July, the island's oldest crafts fair, the **Barranquitas Artisans Fair**, gets underway in the hometown of Puerto Rican patriot Luis Muñoz Rivera, while the **Festival de Santiago Apóstol** in Loíza reflects that town's strong African traditions.

The Club Náutico de San Juan hosts the **International Billfish Tournament**, in August, in which fishermen from around the world seek blue marlin up to 900lb (410kg).

SEPTEMBER – DECEMBER

The **Puerto Rico Symphony**, founded in 1956, kicks off another annual season; later on comes the three-week **Inter-American Festival of the Arts**.

In October, the **Puerto Rico Ten-** nis Open, a women's tennis tournament, is held at San Juan's Central Park, followed later in the month by the **San Juan Cinemafest**, a two-week festival of foreign films.

Each November, Puerto Rico celebrates its Taíno Indian heritage with the **Jayuya Indian Festival**. This colorful event includes craft shows, Indian ceremonies, folk dances and visits to Indian burial sites. Also in November is the **Puerto Rican Day of Bomba y Plena** in Ponce, a celebration of Afro-Caribbean rhythms and dances.

In mid-December, more than 60,000 people attend the **Bacardí Artisans Fair**, held at the Bacardí rum distillery. The year ends, of course, with **Christmas**, when life-size nativity scenes and all-night *parandas* (house-to-house carols) take place everywhere.

Enjoying the salsa rhythm

Practical Information

GETTING THERE

By Air

San Juan's **Luis Muñoz Marín International Airport** is the Caribbean hub for **American Airlines**; as such, American has about 70 percent of all air traffic into and out of the island. Other carriers are Carnival, Delta, US Air, Kiwi, TWA, Iberia, Northwest, United and Viasa. Direct flights link San Juan with Miami, New York (JFK), Boston, Washington, Chicago, Dallas, Atlanta and Caracas, as well as the following European cities: London, Paris, Frankfurt and Madrid.

Flights to the islands of Culebra and Vieques (operated by **Vieques Air Link, Flamenco Airways, Sunaire Express**) leave from San Juan's Isla Grande Airport.

A new fixed-rate system for airport cabs has been introduced. The fare from Luis Muñoz Marin airport to Isla Verde (Zone 1) is $8, to Condado or Miramar (Zone 2) $12 and to Old San Juan and the cruise ship piers (Zone 3) $16.

By Sea

San Juan is a major cruise-ship port. Each year more than a million cruise passengers visit the island. All major Caribbean shipping lines call on San Juan, including Royal Caribbean, which operates two of the largest cruise vessels – *Monarch of the Seas* and *Sovereign of the Seas*. Taxis from the docks to Old San Juan and Puerta de Tierra cost $6, to Condado or Miramar $10, and to Isla Verde, $16.

TRAVEL ESSENTIALS

Visas and Passports

American citizens do not need passports or visas to travel between the US mainland and Puerto Rico, since all such flights are considered domestic. For non-US citizens, visa requirements to enter Puerto Rico are the same as those for visiting anywhere else in the United States.

A sign of noble antecedents

Customs

No customs duties are applied to articles bought in Puerto Rico and taken to the continental United States. It is forbidden, however, to transport potted plants and certain fruits such as mangos, parchas and others to the mainland; all passengers boarding flights back to US cities must pass through a US Department of Agriculture inspection.

Weather

Puerto Rico's climate is among the most pleasant in the world, with San Juan temperatures hovering around 85–90°F (29–32°C) and rarely dipping below 70°F (21°C). It's cooler in the mountainous interior, where you may need a sweater at night. The rainy season peaks in August; average monthly rainfall is 7in (18cm), but when it rains, it rarely lasts for more than a few minutes. The hurricane season – which few Puerto Ricans took seriously until Hurricane Hugo visited the island in 1989 – lasts from May to October.

Clothing

Island dress is very casual, with jeans and knit trousers perfectly acceptable; shorts are less common than on the mainland. Older men frequently don loose-fitting embroidered shirts called *guayaberas,* but it's far more common to see business executives dressed in suits and ties. Cool summer dresses are appropriate for women. The tendency is to dress up for casinos and evening activities.

Time Zones and Electricity

Puerto Rico is located in the Atlantic Time Zone, four hours behind GMT and one hour ahead of New York, Miami and other East Coast cities. In summer, there's no time difference between Puerto Rico and the US East Coast, since Puerto Rico does not observe Daylight Saving Time. Thus 12 noon in Puerto Rico is 8am in California, 4pm in London and midnight in Singapore (but not in summer!) The island also uses standard US electric current; European appliances will need an adaptor.

GETTING ACQUAINTED

Geography

The smallest and easternmost of the Greater Antilles, Puerto Rico covers 3,459sq miles (8,963sq km) and measures 100 miles long by 35 miles wide (160km by 56km). Puerto Rico also includes three offshore islands: Culebra and Vieques to the east, and uninhabited Mona Island to the west. About three-quarters of Puerto Rico is mountainous; the highest peak, Cerro de Punta is 4,390ft (1,338m).

Fun in the sun

Population

With 3.8 million inhabitants, Puerto Rico is one of the world's most densely populated places. Some 1.5 million live in San Juan and its suburbs. Other major urban centers are Ponce, Mayagüez, Caguas, Arecibo and Aguadilla.

Language

Puerto Rico's official languages are Spanish and English.

Government and Economy

Puerto Rico is a US commonwealth whose residents are US citizens and receive most of the benefits and obligations that come with citizenship, including military service. But they can't vote for president and aren't represented in Congress. On the other hand, they are generally not subject to federal income tax.

The economy is heavily oriented toward manufacturing. Section 936, a US job-creating clause partially exempts American companies from paying federal income tax on their Puerto Rico operations. As a result, gross domestic product exceeds $25 billion, and per-capita income is about $7,000. The service sector, including tourism, plays a key role in the economy, as does construction. Agriculture, once the island's economic mainstay, now comprises less than 3 percent of GDP, as sugar, coffee and tobacco exports have shriveled.

Religion

As elsewhere in Latin America, the vast majority of people are Catholic, though Protestant evangelist movements are becoming popular. San Juan has Jewish and Muslim communities of about 2,000 each. For more details, call the Archdiocese of San Juan (tel: 727 7373); Centro Islamico de Puerto Rico (215 Padre Colón, Río Piedras; tel: 766 1235); Jewish Community Center of Puerto Rico (903 Ponce de León, Santurce; tel: 724 4157), or the Second Union Church of Guaynabo (non-denominational services in English; Alto Apolo y E Mileto; tel: 720 4423).

MONEY MATTERS

Currency

The currency is the US dollar (frequently referred to here as the *peso*). Quarters are called *pesetas,* and pennies, *centavos.* Facilities for changing foreign currency are very limited; in Old San Juan, the best place is **Caribbean Exchange** (201-B Calle Tetuán; tel: 722 8222). At the airport, try **Deak International** (tel: 791 1960, 791 2233) and in Santurce, **Banco Popular International Division** (Ponce de León at Calle Europa; tel: 723 0077).

Credit Cards

All major credit cards, including Visa, MasterCard, American Express, Diner's Club and Discover, are accepted throughout the island, but gasoline credit cards generally are not.

Tipping

Generally, 10–15 percent is adequate. In tourist areas, some restaurants add a 15 percent service charge to the bill.

GETTING AROUND

Puerto Rico has more than a million vehicles, but that doesn't mean that it is easy to get around. The public transportation network is inadequate, traffic jams are all too common, and parking is a nightmare – especially in Old San Juan. But renting a car is still the best way to see the island. With more than 8,000 miles (12,900km) of paved roads, no place is more than three hours' drive away.

If you opt for public transportation, there are two choices: buses and *publicos* (mini-vans). The Metropolitan Bus Authority (MBA) operates in the San Juan metro area; buses are air-conditioned and cost 25 cents a ride. Stops are clearly marked by magenta, orange and white *parada* signs. In Old San Juan, buses leave from two terminals: the Covadonga Parking Lot for long routes and Plaza Colón for short ones. For more information, call the MBA at 767 7979 or the Metrobus system at 763 4141.

Publicos generally charge $1 per passenger within the metro area. Major pick-up points include the Río Piedras plaza, Stop 18 in Santurce and Old San Juan's Plaza Colón. Out on the island, *publicos* operate during the day and leave from the town plaza.

Car Hire

San Juan has more than a dozen car-rental agencies to choose from, most with offices at the airport or in nearby Isla Verde. To rent a car you must be at least 25 years old, and hold a major credit card and a valid US or international driver's license. The biggest companies are: **Afro** (tel: 724 3720, 723 8287); **Avis** (tel: 721 4499, 791 0426); **Budget** (tel: 791 3685); **Charlie** (tel: 728 2418, 728 2420); **Discount** (tel: 726 1460, 726 5930); **Hertz** (tel: 791 0840, 791 0844); **L&M** (tel: 725 8307, 725 8416); **Leaseway** (tel: 791 5900, 791 1443); **National** (tel: 791 1805, 791 1851); **Target** (tel: 783 6592, 782 6381).

License to travel

Taxis

Outside the cruise ship docks and airport, where taxis adhere to fixed tariffs, all rates are metered. The initial charge is $1, with each piece of luggage over two pieces 50c and each third of a mile 10c. Taxis can be rented for $20 an hour; night tariffs are $1 extra. Tourist taxis are white and sport the sentry-box logo. Drivers generally speak English as well as Spanish.

The main taxi companies in San Juan are **Major** (tel: 723 1300/723 2460) and **Rochdale** (tel: 721 1900/721 1955). Both have 24-hour service. For limousines, try **Airport Limousine Service** (tel: 791 4745).

Rivera); **25 July** (Constitution Day); **5 September** (Labor Day); **12 October** (Columbus Day); **11 November** (Veterans' Day); **19 November** (Discovery of Puerto Rico); **3rd Thursday in November** (Thanksgiving Day) and **25 December** (Christmas Day).

Bicycles

Puerto Rico has never been known as a bicyclist's paradise, though the municipality of San Juan has developed some bike trails around the Condado and Puerta de Tierra. As locals will tell you, the best way to see Old San Juan is still on foot.

Water Transportation

Ferries operate from Pier 2 in Old San Juan to Cataño. They depart every 30 minutes between 6am and 9pm (tel: 788 1155 for details). Scheduled ferry service also links Fajardo, Vieques and Culebra on a daily basis. For more information, tel: 863 0852.

HOURS AND HOLIDAYS

Business Hours

Business hours follow the US rather than the Latin tradition, and the afternoon *siesta* is generally not practiced. Most stores are open 9am–6pm, banks Monday to Friday, 9am–2.30pm. The **Pueblo** supermarket in Old San Juan is open til 10pm nightly, and the Pueblo de Diego (in the Condado) is open 24 hours a day, seven days a week.

Public Holidays

Puerto Rico is said to have more official days off than anywhere else in the world, thanks to a slew of local and Catholic as well as federally mandated holidays. Some of the minor ones are celebrated as half-day holidays only.

Here are all of them: **1 January** (New Year's Day); **6 January** (Three Kings' Day); **10 January** (Birth of Eugenio Maria de Hostos); **17 January** (Martin Luther King Day); **21 February** (George Washington's Birthday); **22 March** (Abolition of Slavery); **1 April** (Good Friday); **18 April** (Birth of José de Diego); **30 May** (Memorial Day); **4 July** (US Independence Day); **18 July** (Birth of Luis Muñoz

ACCOMMODATIONS

Within the San Juan metro area, major hotel resorts are concentrated in Condado and Isla Verde. These hotels generally feature casinos, live entertainment, business centers, discotheques, fine restaurants, bars and sports facilities. For a lot less, you can stay in any one of a number of guest houses and smaller establishments throughout Condado or Ocean Park. Pricing categories, based on the cost of a double room in the winter season, are as follows:

$ = less than $100
$$ = $100–200
$$$ = $200–300
$$$$ = more than $300

Condado

CONDADO PLAZA HOTEL & CASINO
999 Ashford
Tel: 721 1000
Centrally located, ideal for business travelers, considered Condado's best hotel. Top-notch restaurants, casino, pool, discotheque and business center. **$$$$**

CONDADO BEACH HOTEL & CASINO
1061 Ashford
Tel: 721 6090
Beautiful mansion on outside, government-owned, poorly kept hotel on the inside. Stay here only in a pinch. **$$$**

DUTCH INN & TOWER
55 Condado
Tel: 721 0810
Moderately priced hotel two blocks from the beach; casino and popular restaurant, The Green House. **$$**

EL CANARIO INN
1317 Ashford
Tel: 722 3861
Charming small hotel near the water; lots of character. **$**

RADISSON AMBASSADOR
1369 Ashford
Tel: 721 7300
Formerly Howard Johnson's, still has famous ice-cream parlor; nice piano bar. **$$**

Isla Verde

SANDS HOTEL & CASINO
Isla Verde
Tel: 791 6100
Beautiful modern full-service hotel, Las Vegas-style entertainment at night. **$$$$**

EL SAN JUAN HOTEL & CASINO
Isla Verde
Tel: 791 1000
Has some of San Juan's best restaurants, including Dar Tiffany and Back Street Hong Kong. **$$$$**

HOLIDAY INN CROWNE PLAZA
Route 187, Km 1.5
Tel: 253 2929
Near Boca de Cangrejos and Piñones public beaches. **$$$**

RITZ CARLTON HOTEL & CASINO
Tel: 751-8470
This 418-room luxury property should be finished by September 1997. **$$$**

Puerta de Tierra

CARIBE HILTON
Calle San Jeronimo
Tel: 721 0303
The 650-room Caribe Hiltons the only

Casa San José

hotel in Puerto Rico with its own private beach. Favorite with VIPs. **$$$$**

RADISSON NORMANDIE
Av Muñoz Rivera
Tel: 729 2929
Stark white hotel shaped like a boat; somewhat antiseptic interior. **$$$**

Old San Juan

CASA SAN JOSÉ
159 San José
Tel: 723 1212
A luxuriously restored 300-year-old mansion with 10 sumptuous rooms. **$$$**

EL ESCENARIO GUEST HOUSE
152 San Sebastián
Tel: 721 5264
Charming 7-room guest house above a lively bar. Rates around $50 include breakfast on rooftop terrace. **$**

GALERIA SAN JUAN
204 Norzagaray
Tel: 722 1808
Art gallery and 8-room guest house in 16th-century mansion restored by local sculptor Jan D'Esopo. **$$**

GRAN HOTEL EL CONVENTO
100 Cristo
Tel: 723 9020
An ancient convent converted in the 1960s into a 100-room hotel. **$$**

HOTEL CENTRAL
202 San José
Tel: 722 2751
Right off Plaza de Armas; caters mainly to black Caribbean islanders on shopping or business trips. **$**

WYNDHAM OLD SAN JUAN HOTEL AND CASINO
La Marina
Old San Juan
This 242-room hotel (to be the old city's largest upon completion) is the cornerstone of the ambitious Paseo Portuario – a $125 million, seven-building development which is supposed to turn Old San Juan's decaying waterfront into a modern showcase of urban planning.

Miramar

HOTEL EXCELSIOR
801 Ponce de León
Tel: 721 7400
Businessman's hotel, easy access to Old San Juan, Condado. $$

HOTEL TORO
605 Miramar
Tel: 725 5150
Nice choice for budget travelers. $

Dorado

HYATT REGENCY CERROMAR DORADO BEACH
Route 693
Tel: 796 1234
Upscale resort with world-renowned golf course and $3 million pool. $$$$

Fajardo

EL CONQUISTADOR RESORT & COUNTRY CLUB
Route 987, Km 4.1
Tel: 863 1000
This newly renovated 918-room resort has everything, including a 100-acre (40-ha) private island accessible by ferry boat. $$$$

Guanica

COPAMARINA BEACH RESORT
PO Box 805
First-class resort hidden among 18 acres of mangrove cays, coconut palms and Guanica's famous dry forest. $$$

Ponce

HOLIDAY INN PONCE
Highway 2, Km 221.2
Tel: 844 1200
Overlooks the Caribbean $$

HOTEL MELIA
2 Cristina
Tel: 842 0260
Charming hotel in heart of restored district. Room price includes breakfast on rooftop terrace. $

PONCE HILTON
Highway 14
Tel: 259 7676 or 259 7777
Government-owned hotel. Has casino and 18-hole golf course. $$

Rincón

HORNED DORSET PRIMAVERA HOTEL
Route 429, km3
Tel: 823-4030
This is Puerto Rico's most luxurious small hotel. It is famous for its gourmet food, antique furnishings, European Service and spectacular sunsets. No children are allowed. $$

Rio Grande

WESTIN RIO MAR
Rio Grande
Upon completion, this 600-room, $175 million property will be one of Puerto Rica's largest luxury resorts. $$$$

Pool-side comfort

Paradores

Out on the island, stay in one of Puerto Rico's wonderful *paradores* or country inns for a different kind of experience. Many of these *paradores* are restored 19th-century coffee plantations, and are located in particularly scenic areas.

Rates are very reasonable, usually not more than $60-80 a night, and the food is often much better than what you'd find at nearby restaurants. From the US mainland, *parador* reservations can be made through a central toll-free number (800) 443 0266. In San Juan, dial 721 2884; from outside the metro area, call (800) 981 7575, which is also toll-free.

At the moment, 18 *paradores* are certified by the Puerto Rico Tourism Company: **Baños de Coamo** (Coamo; tel: 825 2239); **Boquemar** (Boquerón; tel: 851 2158); **Casa Grande** (Utuado; tel: 894

3939); **El Faro** (Aguadilla; tel: 822 8000);
Sol (Mayagüez; tel: 834 0303); **Guajataca**
(Quebradillas; tel: 895 3070); **Hacienda
Gripiñas** (Jayuya; tel: 828 1717); **Ha-
cienda Juanita** (Maricao; tel: 838 2550);
J B Hidden Village (Aguada; tel: 886
8686); **Joyuda Beach** (Boquerón; tel: 851
5650); **La Familia** (Fajardo; tel: 863
1193); **Martorell** (Luquillo; tel: 889
2710); **Oasis** (San Germán; tel: 892 1175);
Perichi's (Rincón; tel: 851 3131); **Posada
Porlamar** (La Parguera; tel: 899 4015);
Villa Antonio (Rincón; tel: 823 2645);
Villa Parguera (La Parguera; tel: 899
3975) and **Vistamar** (Quebradillas; tel:
895 2065).

EMERGENCIES
Hospitals

Emergency health care is cheaper in Puerto
Rico than on the US mainland, and hospitals are generally equipped with the latest medical technology. In the tourist areas,
major hospitals include **Ashford Pres-
byterian Community Hospital** in the
Condado (tel: 721 2160); **Hato Rey Community Hospital** (tel: 754 0909) and **Hospital Auxilio Mutuo** (tel: 758 2000) in
Hato Rey; **Hospital San Carlos** (tel: 727
5858), **Hospital San Jorge** (tel: 727 1000)
and **Hospital Pavia** (tel: 727 6060) in
Santurce, and **Hospital San Pablo** (tel:
747 4747) in Bayamón.

Pharmacies

In Old San Juan, try **Walgreen's** (tel: 722
6290) or **Puerto Rico Drug** (tel: 725
2202), both located on the Plaza de Armas. Walgreen's also has a 24-hour location on Ashford Avenue in the Condado
(tel: 725 1510).

Emergency Services

Despite some technical problems Puerto
Rico now has an islandwide 911 phone
system to handle all police, fire and medical emergencies. Dispatchers generally un-
derstand English.

Safety

Crime is a major concern in Puerto Rico,
especially in low income areas where violence and drug use are prevalent. Car-

Familiar sign

jacking is on the increase (though this is
less of a concern away from the big cities).
For your own security, drive with windows up and doors locked in the metro
area, and lock your car when unattended.

To report a crime, call **911** or contact
the Puerto Rico Tourist Zone Police on
Vieques Street in the Condado (open 24
hours a day, seven days a week; tel: 722
0738 or 724 5210).

Complaints

If you have problems of any kind, contact the Puerto Rico Tourism Company
at 721 2400 (in Ponce, tel: 840 5695).

COMMUNICATIONS AND NEWS
Postal Services

The main post offices and philatelic bu-
reaus are in Old San Juan (tel: 723 1277)
and in Hato Rey (tel: 767 2890). Two-day
Priority Mail service is available and
overnight documents can be sent via Federal Express (tel: 793 9300). United Par-
cel Service and DHL also have offices here.

Telecommunications

Puerto Rico has a nearly 100 percent dig-
ital telephone network, with clear and easy
connections to the US mainland and elsewhere. Pay-phone calls still cost only a
dime; AT&T, MCI and Sprint cards all work
from here. The area code is in the process of changing from 809 to 787; after
January 31, 1997, the use of 787 will be

mandatory when calling the island. Long-distance calls within Puerto Rico require dialing only the 7-digit number, but beware: a 3-minute call from San Juan to Mayagüez costs more than calling Los Angeles. For calls to destinations outside the United States, Canada and neighboring islands, dial **011** followed by the country code and phone number.

Media

Puerto Rico has a choice of three daily newspapers, all of them tabloids: *El Vocero* (circulation 240,000), *El Nuevo Día* (200,000) and *The San Juan Star* (circulation 33,000 and the island's only English-language daily). There's also the weekly *El Diario* (it started out as a daily, hence the name) and the *Claridad* (official organ of the independence movement). The English-language *Caribbean Business* provides weekly economic coverage.

In addition, the following newspapers are flown in daily and sold at major newsstands: *The New York Times*, *The Miami Herald*, *El Nuevo Herald*, *The Wall Street Journal*, *The Financial Times* and an assortment of dailies from Italy and Spain.

Puerto Rico has more than 100 radio stations, including the English-language WOSO (1030 on the AM dial), which provides hourly news, weather and sports. In eastern Puerto Rico, English-language stations can be received from the Virgin Islands. Puerto Rico also has half a dozen TV stations of its own.

MUSEUMS AND GALLERIES

Aguadilla en San Juan (205 Cruz; tel: 722 0578); **Corrine Timsit International Gallery** (104 San José; tel: 724 1039); **Estudio Serrano** (353 San Francisco; tel: 722 7652); **Fenn Studio/Gallery** (58 San José; tel: 725 0361); **Galería Botello** (208 Cristo; tel: 723 2879); **Galería Calibán** (51 Cristo; tel: 722 4443); **Galería Coabey** (101 San José; tel: 723 1395); **Galería del Puerto** (Plazoleta del Puerto; tel: 723 4622); **Galería José E Alegria** (154 Cristo; tel: 721 8092); **Galería Leonora Vega** (202 Fortaleza; tel: 723 0043); **Galería Liga de Arte** (San José; tel: 722 4468); **Galería Luigi Marrozzini** (156 Cristo;

tel: 725 2840); **Galería Palomas** (207 Cristo; tel: 724 8904); **Galería Sol** (109 Sol); **Galería W Labiosa** (200 Cristo; tel: 721 2848); **Galería San Juan** (204 Norzagaray; tel: 722 1808); **La Princesa Building** (La Puntilla; tel: 721 2400); **Mariangel Galería/Cuna de Museo** (500 Norzagaray; tel: 722 3081); **Museo del Niño** (Children's Museum), 150 Cristo, San Juan; Tuesday to Thursday 9.30am–3.30pm, weekends 11am–4pm; tel: 722 3791; **Museum of Contemporary Puerto Rican Art** (Edif Barat, Sacred Heart University, off Ponce de León, Santurce; weekdays 9am–4pm; tel: 268 0049); **Caparra Ruins** and **Museum of the Conquest and Colonization of Puerto Rico** (Highway 2, Km 6.6, Bayamón; daily 9am–4pm; tel: 781 4795); **Francisco Oller Art and History Museum** (off Bayamón Plaza; weekdays 8am–noon and 1–4pm; tel: 798 8191); **José Celso Barbosa Museum** (Route 167 near Bayamón Plaza; weekdays 8am–noon; tel: 798 8191); **Luis A Ferré Science Park** (museums of geology/physical sciences, archaeology and natural sciences), Route 167 south of De Diego Expressway; Wednesday to Friday 8am–4pm, weekends 10am–6pm; tel: 740 6868; **Historical Museum of Caguas**, (weekdays 8am–3pm; tel: 746 0669); **University of Puerto Rico Museum of Anthropology, History and Art** (Ponce de León, Río Piedras; weekdays 9am–9pm, Saturday 8am–3.30pm; tel: 764 0000).

USEFUL INFORMATION

Bookstores

Bell Book & Candle (102 De Diego, Santurce; tel: 728 5000); **Bookworld** (Plaza Las Américas, Hato Rey; tel: 753 7140); **Casa Papyrus** (also has a music store and coffee shop), 357 Tetuán, Old San Juan, tel: 724 6555); **The Book Store** (255 San José, Old San Juan; tel: 724 1815); **Thekes Inc** (Plaza Las Américas, Hato Rey; tel: 765 1539).

Some you win…

Gambling

Casinos are in all the major hotels, though the best are at **El San Juan**, the **Sands**, the **Condado Plaza**, the **Condado Beach** and the **Caribe Hilton**. Outside the metropolitan area, try **El Conquistador**, the **Hyatt Regency Cerromar Beach Hotel**, the **Ponce Hilton**, the **Mayagüez Hilton** and **Palmas del Mar**.

Gay Visitors

The center of gay life is **Calle Vendig** in the Condado. The **Atlantic Beach Hotel** (1 Vendig; tel: 721 6900) and its **Seabreeze Restaurant** caters specifically to homosexuals; so do the **Ocean Walk Guest House** (1 Atlantic Place; tel: 728 0855) and the **Embassy Guest House** (1126 Sea View; tel: 725 2400). Gay/lesbian discos include **Krash** (1257 Ponce de León; 722 1390); **Lazer's** (215 Cruz, Old San Juan; tel: 721 4479) on Thursday and Sunday nights, and **Skydance** (Calle Recinto Sur, Old San Juan) on Monday nights.

USEFUL ADDRESSES

Tourism Information

On the US mainland, call the **Puerto Rico Tourism Company** toll-free at (800) 223 6530. Outside the United States:
Canada: 41–3 Colbourne Street, Toronto, Ontario, M5E1E3. Tel: 368-2680.
France: 5 Bis, Rue de Louvre, 75001, Paris. Tel: 44 77 88 00.

Hold your horses

Germany: Abraham Lincoln Strasse 2, 65189, Weisbaden. Tel: (611) 9772312.
Italy: Via Dante 2/53, 15121, Genoa. Tel: 553-1169.
Spain: Calle Serrano 1, 28001 Madrid. Tel: 431-2128.

Consulates

Canada, Scotiabank Plaza, Piso 13, Hato Rey, tel: 250 0367.
France, Edif Mercantil Plaza 720, Hato Rey, tel: 753 1700
Germany, Santa Bibliana 1618, Río Piedras, tel: 755 8228.
Italy, Amatista 93, Río Piedras, tel: 793 5284.
Spain, Edif Mercantil Plaza, Hato Rey, tel: 758 6090.
UK, Taft 1, 5-E, Condado, tel: 728 6715.

FURTHER READING

Insight Guide: Puerto Rico Apa Publications. Hong Kong (1996). Background essays, travel tips and a comprehensive run-down of places.
Puerto Rico: A Colonial Experiment Carr, Raymond. New York: Random (1984).
Puerto Rico: A Political and Cultural History Carrión, Arturo Morales (editor). New York: W W Norton (1982).
The Puerto Ricans: A Documentary History Wagenheim, Kal and Jiménez de Wagenheim, Olga (editors). Princeton: Marcus Wiener Publishing (1993).

Índex

ACKNOWLEDGMENTS

Photography	Bill Wassman *and*
91	Caribe Hilton
11, 12T & B	reproduced from *Historia de Puerto Rico*
	by Salvador Brau
15, 32, 48, 54, 69T & B	Larry Luxner
Production Editor	Mohammed Dar
Handwriting	V.Barl
Cover Design	Klaus Geisler
Cartography	Berndtson & Berndtson